What people are saying about…

OVERCOMING
Mediocrity©

5 out of 5 Stars

It's a Great Investment in Yourself

"This is an inspiring compilation. Each woman's story contains powerful lessons that are widely applicable. Heartwarming and triumphant all at the same time. Any woman who's tread a rocky path on her life's journey will be able to relate and rejoice along with each author as she overcomes adversity and challenge. If you're seeking inspiration to overcome adversity, take a moment to breathe, regroup, and soak up a story or three. It's a great investment in yourself."

—Debbra

5 out of 5 Stars

Highly Recommend!!

"HIGHLY RECOMMEND!!! If you are looking for personal and professional development, this book is for you! It is perfectly inspiring, educational, empowering and beautifully written! I could really relate to the struggles in their personal stories and it has helped me to continue working on overcoming my own obstacles so I can succeed in life and in business! Thank you all for sharing your incredible journeys."

—Lisa

5 out of 5 Stars

Inspired, Raw Stories from the Heart

"Inspiring! As someone who cares about helping people in a purposeful way, I continually find myself reminded that everyone has a story. What is unique about "Resilient Women Overcoming Mediocrity" is that each woman's (life) chapter differs in remarkable ways- their family dynamics, circumstances, and work experiences - and yet chose the option of going into business for themselves (often despite immense odds) and came out remarkable well on the other side.

Through raw sharing, they willingly own their history-no easy feat! I highly recommend this book for any woman who is looking for support, another way, or camaraderie and who may struggle in her own path; someone who finds inspiration from others who have overcome often great challenges and have paved the way for the rest of us. There is a difference between mediocrity and adversity. These authors have set the bar to overcome both. Kudos to all."

— Brenda

4 out of 5 Stars

A Book of Empowering and Inspiring Stories by Women!

"This book is full of amazing stories of women who have overcome adversity in different ways. They have gone above and beyond the usual and succeeded in discovering their talents and power to do whatever they put their minds to. These incredible women display a strength of character and stamina and perseverance needed in a tough competitive world. I found this book to be inspiring and quite enjoyable. The women each have different personalities but there is one thread that is the same - their determination to succeed in their chosen fields.

I would recommend this book to all women whether they are in business or not to help them believe in themselves - believe that even the impossible is possible!"

— Jjspina

5 out of 5 Stars

This Book Is Great! It Really Motivated Me.

"This book is great! It really motivated me to take the next step with my life and career. All of these women have accomplished so much, and I strive to be like them. We can all achieve greatness if we put in a little effort!"

—Amazon Customer

5 out of 5 Stars

Excellent Read for Men and Women!

"LOVED THE BOOK! [Husband] thought it should not be limited to a "women's" book – excellent for men and women. Writing was personal, intimate, yet clearly educational in nature. Long enough to take you somewhere, but short enough to sit down and read right then. The book is downloaded on our Kindle so we can read again."

—TJ

5 out of 5 Stars

Hope and Faith

"I loved this very inspirational book. All of the women had such different stories. I ordered another copy for a Christmas gift. It's exactly what we all need to remind us that we can overcome with faith."

—Amazon Customer

OVERCOMING MEDIOCRITY

VICTORIOUS WOMEN

OVERCOMING

Mediocrity©

**A unique collection of stories from victorious women
who have created their own lives of significance!**

Presented by Christie L. Ruffino

DPWN Publishing

www.OvercomingMediocrity.org

This book is a compilation of stories from numerous experts who have each contributed a chapter. It is designed to provide information and inspiration to our readers.

It is sold with the understanding that the publisher and the individual authors are not engaged in the rendering of psychological, legal, accounting or other professional advice. The content and views in each chapter are the sole expression and opinion of its author and not necessarily the views of DPWN Publishing, Christie Lee Ruffino or the Dynamic Professional Women's Network, Inc.

For more information, contact:
DPWN Publishing
A division of the Dynamic Professional Women's Network, Inc.
1879 N. Neltnor Blvd. #316, West Chicago, IL 60185
www.OvercomingMediocrity.org
www.OurDPWN.com

Printed in the United States of America

ISBN: 978-1-939794-15-4

Dedication

To every woman who does not believe she can make a difference and to every woman who believes she can move a mountain.

To every woman who continually makes sacrifices for those she loves and to every woman who prioritizes those moments when she can pamper and take care of her own needs.

To every woman who believes that she should settle for the life she has and to every woman who has overcome great odds to create her own life of significance.

To the resilient women in this book who have shared their stories with you in hopes that their lessons of pain will become your lessons of power.

To the women in my life who believe I am significant and whom I believe are priceless.

The Power of a Story

There is nothing more important in this world than the relationships we build and the legacy we leave in the lives of those who have crossed paths with us on our journey of life. It's the experiences we have along this journey that define our individual uniqueness and creates our own powerful personal blueprint or our unique story snowflake.

It is this blueprint that can empower us to possess a distinct advantage over every other person in this world if leveraged correctly and shared. If we don't have the courage to share our snowflake, it will be lost forever. No one will have the same story and no one can repeat your story. Therefore, those who come after you will never learn anything from what you experienced and what you learned.

I feel that the most significant thing we can do to add value back into this world is to master the narrative of our lives. All of our leadership and moneymaking abilities rest in our ability to discover, craft and deliver our personal story or message in a way that will allow people to connect to us. The right story shared at the right time with the right person can alter the trajectory of their life.

We also have the ability to learn from other people's stories and change the direction of the stories we are living to shape our ultimate destinies.

Power to you and the story of your life!

"The two most important days in your life are the day you are born and the day you find out why."

—Mark Twain

Introduction

When I embarked upon this journey, to help women share their stories in a book, never in my wildest dreams did I expect it to turn out as it has. My motives were grand, yet much more simplistic than they are today.

My initial goal was to create one collaborative book, collecting stories from the women I admired who were members of the Dynamic Professional Women's Network (DPWN). I knew that when I had shared my story in a similar book compiled by a mentor of mine, Michelle Prince, the experience had been transformational for me. I also knew that having a book to share in the business community gave me additional credibility, recognition and exposure. What I didn't know was that these same stories would be just as transformational for the readers, as they related with one or more of the women who were willing to share their stories in such a vulnerable and authentic way.

I also had no way of knowing how working with these women would lead me down a path that would change my life forever...

My Journey

I'm a natural connector. Most women are, actually. I believe it's part of our DNA to bring people together with other people or resources that can help them. Many times, I've shared that my journey to build the Dynamic Women's Professional Network, Inc. was not intentional. As an introvert, the last thing I wanted to do was to build a business where I would have to talk with new people all of the time. But thankfully, God knew better than I did what was best for me.

Now, 13 years later, our community is still thriving in the Chicagoland area. Our *Overcoming Mediocrity* series of books is going just as strong, celebrating book number seven, featuring an amazing lineup of victorious women. The stories in these books are about strength, faith, and courage. They are about having the confidence to believe in ourselves, even when those we love don't. They are about having the courage to do things that are hard, even when we may not want to. And they are about remaining resilient through all of life's ups and downs because that is what, as women, we do brilliantly.

Another Life Changing Moment

It was just a few days before Christmas, and I headed to a local hardware store to get the final parts to a project I was working on. No sooner did I turn from the Customer Service Counter, only to trip and go went flying, because a long metal piece of sheet-metal was obstructing my path. I felt embarrassed and tried to get up before anyone saw me... but I couldn't. I had really gotten hurt. My knee and my elbow were in excruciating pain. I thought the pain would pass and that I could fight through it, get up, and make my way back home. I had so much to do to get ready for Christmas, and I had a brand-new program that was on the verge of launching.

I had to keep working!!! If I didn't work, I couldn't pay my bills or the long list of business expenses that kept accumulating. I would feel better in the morning... And heck, I couldn't let a silly fall stop me from making things happen.

But when I attempted to get up, I realized that my hand hurt just as badly. I couldn't get up! And if I could somehow get up, I could never walk on my leg. It hurt too FREAKING bad!

I had to accept assistance from a passing customer just to get off the floor and into a wheelchair. And, more importantly, I had to accept that my plans for the next few weeks—or possibly the next few months—were going to be completely OUT OF MY CONTROL.

Have you ever been rolling through life when something unexpected stopped you in your tracks and sent you down another road, a road that you had no intention of taking? Of course you have... Most of us have.

- How long did it take for you to accept that new direction?

- Did you succumb quickly, or did you fight it every step of the way?

- What did you learn from going down that new road?

For seven years I've worked with hundreds of women, helping them not only to share their stories, but to determine what to share and how best to share it. It's been a great experience for me—I just love helping women accomplish their big dreams!

But, do you know what I don't love? I don't love knowing that some of them never did anything with their newly acquired Amazon Bestselling Author status. Or that they finally published a book, but all of the copies are still sitting in a box in their basement.

Many of them did leverage their books, and their businesses are growing. That's what they wanted, and they are happy to reap that reward.

However, some of their businesses are skyrocketing. They're exceeding their goals. What are they doing that the other women didn't?

That's exactly what I discovered during the most recent chapter of my story, when life as I knew it came screeching to a halt. My busy schedule was wiped clean, and swapped out with long days of pain, overwhelm and feelings of being completely lost.

Okay… I didn't actually just discover it. It was there all along. I just couldn't see it before, because my days were so busy that I was not able to see things objectively. It's like when we return home after a long vacation, only to become instantly aware of the one-inch layer of ceiling fan dust, the disgustingly dirty windows and the overloaded refrigerator with far too many outdated condiments. They are all just as you left them only days prior; it's just that seeing them with fresh eyes creates new objectivity.

Your Journey

We all have a plethora of stories that can be leveraged for various reasons. Only when we are able to discover our true purpose in life, and we share the story that led us down the road to discover that purpose, are we able to make the biggest impact.

And when we share that story, we have to do more than just write about our journey. We need to create a fluid document that will transform people's lives! Whether it is a book, or a chapter in a book, we need to follow a formula that will serve our audience at the highest level.

- What is your big mission in life?
- Do you know who your ideal client avatar is and how you can best serve them?
- Do you know what makes you the expert in this area and the go-to leader in your industry?
- Have you identified your unique Personal Power Story?
- Do you know what sub-stories will take your audience on a journey to connect with you and learn from you?

If you answered yes to all of these questions, then congratulations! You are on the right road. I challenge you to stay the course and not get distracted by shiny new adventures.

If you are in doubt and lack clarity on any of those questions, I challenge you to find someone to help you figure it out. Quit wasting time trying to figure it out on your own. Although the DIY path will save you money, you will waste months or even years of your precious time.

You have the power to change lives with your story, but you have to step out of your own way to make it happen. It's FREAKING scary!!! It most definitely is. But if you don't step out of your comfort zone, you will always be in the same place… going down the same road.

You have a choice—you really do. It's your time to say "YES" to being seen as the go-to expert in your industry. It's time to attract a bigger audience of prospects who will see you as the answer to their problems, and a loyal community of clients who will want more from you and will love referring business to you. It's time to finally have the satisfaction of being able to help your clients make HUGE transformational shifts in their lives.

Your future is totally up to you! Choose the best road, before life makes you take a road you don't want. You don't have to believe me… you simply have to believe in yourself!

Our Book Series

Our first *Overcoming Mediocrity* book was a smashing success! On the very first day of its release in 2013, it became the #1 downloaded Kindle book in the motivational genre category. Twenty-two women shared their stories to inspire other women to overcome and succeed as they had, and all authors were able to claim the distinguished Amazon Bestselling Author status.

Because of the overwhelming success of that first book, we went on to produce additional books under the *Overcoming Mediocrity* brand. Each of them also climbed to the #1 position on Amazon on the very first day of release. Our last two books, *Overcoming Mediocrity—Resilient Women* and *Influential Women,* both reached the #1 position in two categories in the same day.

This series of books have ultimately taken on a life of their own and have made a greater impact than ever anticipated. It is exciting to read testimonials from women who have read one of the books and connected with the inspirational stories inside. It is even more exciting when one of those same women decides to share her story in one of our future books.

And now, it is with great honor and pride that I am able to share stories from the victorious women in this book. I have had the pleasure of getting to know each of these ladies and learning a little about the stories they're sharing with you. I'm deeply inspired by the courage they're exhibiting. They are sharing the personal details of their lives with the sole intention of allowing you, the reader, to learn from their experiences.

It is easy to become complacent and live a mediocre life, but these women made a choice to live lives of significance. Now they share their lives with you throughout the pages of this book. This demonstrates courage and strength, as well as humility and the heart of a true go-giver. These women all have even greater things yet to come. They are women whom you should know, learn from, and emulate.

This book is meant to not only encourage you, but also to awaken you to recognizing the true value of collaboration. The women in this book want to make the biggest possible impact on the world and transform as many lives as possible, by sharing their stories in a book that will get massive exposure. They could have kept their stories private; that would have been the safest and easiest path for them. But they decided to step out of their comfort zones and share the narratives of their lives with you.

I am blessed to have the opportunity to share this book with you. I hope you feel just as blessed to receive the value these women and their stories offer you.

Hugs & Blessings,

Christie

Table of Contents

Jeanie Martin

We've Unleashed Her

Today, I want to tell you a story. It's a story about me, Jeanie, the consultant who wanted to become a National Sales Director. I love reading books to my grandchildren, and one of my favorite books to read when Avery and Skylar came to my house was about Charlie the Caterpillar, who changes into a beautiful butterfly. Charlie's butterfly story only takes about 22 pages, and my Mary Kay story encompasses almost 22 years.

Charlie's story was written so little readers would learn from his experiences, and my story might be told so you "older kids" could benefit from my experiences and the wisdom I've gained. We are all in the process of writing our own life story, yet we aren't always conscious of what chapter we're composing. Are you wallowing or are you soaring? Could your story be a best seller, or better left unread? Like me, do you have life lessons you want to share?

If I were going to tell you my victory story, I'd start with the August day in 1988 that I joined Mary Kay and ordered a whole lot of inventory. I was wearing cutoff blue jeans and had never had a Mary Kay product on my face. I was being interviewed by a woman in a drop-dead gorgeous designer dress who'd driven to my house in a pink Cadillac. Some people may not have recognized that I was going to grow up to be an awesome butterfly. Most importantly, I didn't realize it. And maybe I didn't think I deserved butterfly status at that time in my life.

I'd been teaching high school English for years, and I liked what I did, but I had always wanted to own my own business. I was teaching Shakespeare and commas, but what jazzed me was seeing kids get fired up about doing what they'd never done before. I thrived on watching kids give dynamic debates and create children's books they'd end up holding onto for years. When I could unlock potential and see that flash of desire to do what it takes to be their best, that's when I got fired up. Looking back, I was making an impact on kids, but my audience was limited to the small rural school where I taught. I had no idea there could be another career that would use my talents. I didn't know I would end up touching thousands of lives across the country with my words. I didn't realize it, but what I was doing was settling, settling for what life had handed me. I needed to be proactive. I needed to see a bigger picture.

I didn't grow up with suggestions to be an entrepreneur, find a vision, and become a leader. I grew up being told to earn a decent salary, have family security, and look forward to retirement. I didn't realize what was out there for butterflies: an unlimited income potential, freedom and flexibility, and untapped leadership potential.

Let's go back to the book and back to my past for just a minute. In the book, Charlie Caterpillar asks some monkeys if he can play with them, and they tell him he is ugly and to "get outta here." When I was in high school, I was the smart one, not the pretty one...badly permed hair, funny-looking glasses, skinny as a rail, no fashion sense at all, and the boys didn't ask me out.

In the book, little Charlie wants to play with some rabbits, and they tell him he is ugly and to "get outta here." When I went to college, I went through rush, and the "good-looking" girls sorority...didn't ask me to join.

Charlie wants to play with a couple of mice, and they tell him he is ugly and to "get outta here." And in a small town I got divorced, and the married couples...they didn't ask me to come along.

And that's when Charlie and I went into our cocoon time. For Charlie, it was only a winter season that passed...it might have been years in my lifetime. When I was growing up, girls became teachers, nurses, or secretaries. I was the first in my family to go to college. I was also the first in my family to get a divorce. I was the first to figure out how to support two kids and pay for a house. Parents always want their kids to have a better life than they did, and I wanted to live up to my parents' unspoken expectations. I got my master's degree, I married an incredible man, we were raising two amazing daughters, I enjoyed teaching high school English, and I was coming out of my cocoon with all the trappings to become an awesome butterfly.

That's when Mary Kay came along. I was making changes, but I needed something more to be the best butterfly I could be. Looking back, to push through to reach my potential, what I needed was confidence and belief, personal and professional skills, and consistent, daily activity.

To get that confidence, I needed friends who thought I was smart, who thought I was pretty, and who wanted to "play" with me. And through Mary Kay, I gained new friendships and developed deep relationships. I entered a whole world filled with caterpillars and butterflies who are now my offspring directors, my area consultants, my clients, and my dearest national friends. Because I had a director who cheered for me when I held an appointment and sold a miracle set, I learned how to genuinely praise people for booking appointments, and to hand out ribbons for selling one hundred dollars in a day. But remember, this didn't happen in a page, in a day, or even in a year; it all took time.

Deep inside, even though I was a bona fide butterfly, a part of me didn't believe it. I would climb the MK ladder a rung, and I'd worry about staying there or going higher. I was always afraid I didn't have what it takes. My confidence felt shaky when I looked at the next rung on that ladder to success.

As I grew up in my Mary Kay world, I thrived on the recognition. The first time I was Queen of our fall quarterly event and sat on a haystack throne, I felt so proud, but for quite a while, I was intimidated by the directors who had won pink Cadillacs. Maybe I was still thinking of the boys in high school who didn't ask me out.

Finally, I realized I needed to keep seeing faces and doing interviews, and I could be like those directors. When I put products on faces and told people about the career opportunity, everything worked. A seemingly insignificant effort, consistently made, was all I needed to do. Success would come if I'd show up and do one face at a time.

When I became a director, I was so in awe of the unit club directors and the Cadillac directors. I knew all their names at the Chicago director meetings and at leadership conferences, but I never talked to them. Maybe I was still thinking about the sorority girls in college who didn't think I added up. Again, my belief was shaky, but I remembered what it took. I filled my datebook for that week and the week after. To get to the next rung, I kept showing up, doing it one face at a time.

And when it worked, and I became a Cadillac director, I was in awe of those trip taking directors. I felt I could never talk to them. Maybe I was still thinking about the married couples in our small town who never asked me to join them when I was single. I didn't let that stop me. I learned new scripts and developed leadership skills, and I kept showing up, adding one face at a time.

And when I became a trip taking director, I was so in awe of those million-dollar directors that I could never talk to them comfortably. They knew so much more, and they did so much more, and it must be an accident that I was on that top director trip. But I learned to stop doubting myself. Instead, I kept showing up, consistently, doing one face at a time, and my belief grew.

And when I finally went on five and six and then seven trips, and our unit did one million, not once but twice, I wondered if I might actually be able to move into the national position. But there are so few nationals, I told myself, and the requirements seem so demanding, and there are so many directors I know who want to be nationals and aren't. How can I even think that I can make it? I didn't let those thoughts stop me. I went back and did one face, adding one new director at a time.

This process of personal growth took years, and there were glorious moments of belief, but for each next step, I had to build new confidence before reaching that next rung.

Let's be clear—in spite of all those worries, I do have stationary that has National Sales Director next to my name, and I do believe I earned and deserve that accolade.

Do any of you think that words from your past are still in your head, and sometimes they stop you from enjoying who you are? Was there ever someone along the way who made you feel you weren't good enough, and you didn't add up? Do you ever worry about getting to the next level and not being able to stay there or climb higher?

Maybe you too have felt uneasy. Maybe you would like to be a caterpillar who evolves. Please allow me to share how Jeanie Consultant, in 22 years, transformed into a magnificent MK National Butterfly.

Way back at the beginning of my story, I mentioned that when a caterpillar transforms into a butterfly, it's a process. I said it took confidence and belief, personal and professional skills, and consistent daily activity.

Let's look back to see how developing skills created energy that generated my caterpillar metamorphosis. One big MK jump was going from consultant in 1988 to director in 1990. My energy came from learning the basic skills of being a consultant and then acting on them. Let me emphasize the take action part. It was not enough to learn the skills; I had to make them part of my routine. I was holding three to five appointments a week, and at that time, I was a full-time high school English teacher who was the National Honor Society advisor, the senior class advisor, and the SADD advisor, and I had two daughters in grade school who were in every sport.

The reward for learning the skills and having consistent daily and weekly activity was I earned money to take my daughters and husband to Rome to visit my brother who was living there. I continued to perfect skills and work diligently. For two years I was on the Queen's Court of Personal Sales and #9 in the Emerald Division, and that meant I was selling about $40,000 worth of product a year and making almost half of that.

As a bonus, I got to wear a sequined gown and pick up a diamond ring on stage. And as I stood at the top of those seminar stairs, I might have remembered those high school boys who never asked me out. As I walked down those seminar steps in front of 10,000 people, and the tuxedoed man on each step took my hand and told me how beautiful I looked, I might have remembered how most of those high school boys are now kind of pudgy and bald...and I grew in confidence as I won my first car and became a director.

As a director, I took on a new role and learned to transfer my skills to others who could make their goals and dreams come true. And when our unit jumped to pink Cadillac status, what did it take? I added recruiting skills and leadership skills and added personal team members and earned bonuses. I remember making a pink car poster, and each consultant filled in her name and her order on the bumper and on the license plate of the poster as I earned the use of that pink Caddie one order, one face at a time. As a reward, our unit had a car party at the dealership, and the dealer had pink cookies and pink punch, and my unit members brought pink balloons, and we all piled in the trunk of that pink Cadillac and took pictures as I signed my name twice and drove out of the showroom with a $40,000 vehicle. As we headed to a restaurant for dinner to celebrate, I thought about all those sorority girls who never chose me. And I wondered how many of their friends joined them when they picked up their last car. And my confidence was growing.

And when I set my sights on earning a trip to Rome...there was a huge surge of energy. Some people might call that energy passion. What I know for sure is that people feel energy and they follow passion. Because I was teaching the skills I learned, sharing my knowledge, and pouring belief and confidence into others, we sold over $750,000 worth of Mary Kay products that year.

During that same year, my daughter, Amy, decided to work her Mary Kay business, and she was a consultant who actually did everything I asked. Not always as a teenager, but as a consultant she did! She took out a loan to order her inventory, booked a power start, drove hours to weekly meetings, squeezed in every event, did faces and faces and brought guests and did three-way interviews, and because she did what I asked, she had great sales and won a car, and my unit saw it all working. They caught the excitement, and they were working too and having their personal successes...and our unit jumped from the $450,000 level to that $750,000 level...and I was going to Rome because we were a unit who were all using our skills, working consistently, and doing it all with passion. How's that for implementing a process that grows a person's belief and creates success?

And by the way, do you think I cared about the married couples who years before didn't ask me to join them? Let me tell you about more rewards!

My husband got so excited when he realized we might actually win a trip to Rome that he promised my unit a party. He would host an Italian night at our house, and we coordinated it with Amy's business debut. There were over 90 people there. We live on a lake, and it was a magical, spectacular July night. There were tiny Italian flags lining the walkways, and delicious Italian foods served by waiters, and sultry Italian music wafting out over the lake, and twinkling Italian lights in the trees, and my son-in-law directed cars, and a golf cart brought the people to the house, some who drove over three hours to be there...and the stars were sparkling on that lake that warm summer night. Amy, pregnant with my first grandchild, gave a speech and said, "Mom, you started MK fifteen years ago to take our family to Rome to see Uncle Jeff. I just hope my MK efforts this year are a little payback and helped send you and Reed back to Rome." What kind of belief do you imagine that night generated?

I feel Amy gave belief to women who couldn't relate to me. She was young and having kids and working MK as a full-time business, and that generated a new belief in the MK opportunity. Other young women in my unit believed, If she can, I can, and they also jumped on board, wanting more, and some consultants worked on leadership skills.

Twenty-one of these consultants became my offspring directors because they held full circle skin care classes, and asked for referrals, and booked from those classes, and they did interviews with their hostesses, and they sponsored new consultants who went to their Pink Boot camps, and the ones going to the top communicated weekly and then daily. As leaders, they transferred these skills and reached heights they could never have imagined. If you've ever experienced this kind of synergy, you revel in the outcome and marvel that you're a part of it. The charter members were these directors and their units.

We'd learned about the IT Factor, and while we had IT, we worked IT. When you have IT, people recognize the positive energy, the contagious enthusiasm, and the relentless drive that takes you to a goal. People want to be a part of IT. That's what we had when we grew a national area. There were about 600,000 consultants in the United States, there were about 9,000 directors, and when I was awarded that position, I was one of just 225 nationals.

We were recognized as the IT National Area, and the Charter IT Girls went to Dallas and stood on the seminar stage in black suits and red high heels, and all of us, along with my grandkids, danced on that stage in front of thousands of people.

How did Charlie become a butterfly, and how did I get to that stage, and into this book about victorious women? How did Charlie Caterpillar—no, I mean, Jeanie Consultant grow into a National Sales Director? John Maxwell's Law of Process says that leaders develop daily...not in a day. Charlie took 22 pages, and I took 22 years. You don't have to take 22 years...but there's something you should know about caterpillars. If you try to help them unravel their cocoon, they're not strong enough to survive. If you ever nudge them off the end of a branch before they are ready to fly, they are going to fall, and they are going to die. Caterpillars get their strength and their beauty from the arduous process of spinning their own cocoon and fighting their way out of it. The struggles they have make them strong enough to take on the obstacles they'll face. You can't shorten the process.

Remember, it's confidence and belief, mixed with personal and professional skill development done daily for a long time. When you learn the skills of your trade, your confidence will grow. As you develop your personal leadership skills, your belief in your own success increases. And those small, seemingly insignificant steps that you take every single day for years, lead you up the rungs to success. Each of you caterpillars out there is unique. It's your journey, your cocoon, your process. Remember that if Charlie had allowed those other animals to make him feel ugly, it wouldn't matter how he looked or what he did…on the inside, he'd still be ugly.

You must believe implicitly and to the core that you're the best you. You must learn the tactical skills, and as a leader implement the necessary strategies to work with others. You must work diligently and consistently for long periods, refusing to give up. Do all of that, and you will be followed. This will generate the activity and create enough energy so you, too, can fly. I know you, too, can be the most beautiful butterfly ever! And then what?

As a national butterfly, I reached the highest level of achievement in the Mary Kay world. I taught classes with 3,000 consultants in the audience and gave speeches to 8,000 at a seminar. I recently retired, and as I left my pink bubble, I moved into a new position of Legacy Leader, where I am bringing all that I have learned to a broader audience.

I closed the flap to my butterfly book, and I've already opened a cover, intending to write a new book. In one chapter, Jeanie the National becomes Jeanie the Motivational Speaker who intentionally provokes you to look for your own version of IT.

I've titled another chapter "Rise Up." I'm facilitating small groups of professional women. For this program, I look for high capacity female leaders who want to rise up and make a greater impact on the world. That's a semester program, and the "graduates" are already writing their own butterfly stories.

How about you? Would you like to write your own story? Do you already have a title? I've got mine: Watch Out World, We've Unleashed Her!

Let's get to know each other, so we can all fly!

Connect with Jeanie Martin at jeanie.martin@gmail.com or www.jeaniemartin.com

Jeanie Martin

When Jeanie Martin taught commas and Shakespeare, she was also teaching high school kids how to stand up in front of their peers, overcome their fears, and be their best. When Jeanie taught skin care and make up artistry, she also introduced women and men to an opportunity to build their own business by developing relationships and improving their own self esteem. In that time, she grew a Mary Kay National Area into an organization of over 1,500 people in 36 states. For her last 7, years her national area averaged $4.5 million in retail sales per year.

Jeanie has bachelor degrees in English and speech, a master's degree in reading, and taught high school speech and English. She began building her MK business in 1988 and was in a leadership position with Mary Kay Cosmetics for over 25 years. Some think she left teaching to sell lipstick. In truth, she found a venue in MK that put her in front of thousands more "grown-up kids" to teach and influence.

In 2010, she reached the highest level of Mary Kay Leadership when she was appointed to the National Sales Director position. To put that in perspective, there are about 600,000 Mary Kay consultants in the United States, over 10,000 directors, and only 225 nationals. In that capacity as a National Sales Director, Jeanie was invited to work with leaders all over the country who own their own business. She coaches, mentors, and leads women to tap out their full potential through the avenue of a business.

Since retiring from Mary Kay in 2018 as a Legacy Leader, Jeanie has continued to impact lives. She specializes in leadership and motivation as well as sales training and image development. She's committed and passionate about working with winners to actualize their full potential.

Jeanie's mission is to teach others how to live richer, more abundant lives. An opportunity to speak gives her a platform for fulfilling this purpose.

Jeanie Martin
Jeanie Martin NSDS
1284 Lake Holiday Drive
Sandwich, IL 60548
815-354-3250
Jeanie.Martin@gmail.com
www.JeanieMartin.com

Laticia Thompson

I Am Not My Hair

Who Am I? Such a simple but powerful question. Many people live a lifetime unable to discover the answer.

One of my favorite quotes, by Bevan Lee, is, "I Am. Two of the most powerful words, for what you put after them shapes your reality." When I ponder my life, I can honestly say that it took several decades for me to understand, articulate and live in my "I Am." When did I finally begin living? When did I truly take my first breath? Take a walk with me.

The Beginning

I grew up during a time when beauty was defined by how well your body resembled the shape of an hour glass, or how close your body measurements came to the infamous numbers that seemed to elude many of us; 36-24-36. Beauty was being wrapped in skin that was lighter than a brown paper bag. The lighter your skin, the prettier you were. There was one other element that pulled it all together: Hair. Long, straight, flowing hair was the icing on the cake. The topper on the tree.

I wanted to be beautiful. At the time I didn't know what beauty was except what society deemed it was. So, I went on a pursuit. I didn't know that the pursuit would result in me achieving the opposite of what I'd longed for.

Becoming the Mask

I was the ripe young age of 10 when I started altering my hair. My parents also wanted my hair to grow, so they allowed me to jump on the hottest hair craze at the time. If you grew up in the 80's you know what I'm talking about. Yep, you guessed it... the Jheri curl. Oh yeah!! I was too cute. I still have the picture my dad took of me the first day I got my Jheri curl. I was standing outside at my grandfather's shop. I was wearing a cute striped tank top and purple shorts, sporting an innocent smile, hands clasped together, with a slight head tilt. I can remember it like it was yesterday. When I think about that picture and how excited I was in that moment about my new hairdo, confidence didn't know me.

After many years of enduring wet shirt collars and greasy pillowcases that caused horrible pimple problems, it was time to move on to the next hair craze: relaxed hair. In the Black community the purpose of the chemical relaxer was to straighten our natural curl pattern; the straighter the better. There's a science to applying the chemical. If not done correctly you could lose your hair. After years of getting my hair relaxed, I began losing it. Heartbreaking!! I had to mask my reality by wearing a bang hair piece that I glued in. Over time, the constant gluing resulted in losing more and more hair. What the heck? I now needed a bigger mask to cover my reality.

So, I got braids. Braids were a low maintenance, easy-to-manage hair style. I thought I'd hit the jackpot. Because I was no longer relaxing my hair, I thought my hair would grow back. Dagnabbit! I was wrong AGAIN. You see, after years and years of pulling and tugging at my hair follicles, I'd permanently damaged them. Over time I'd lost all of my hair in the front, and eventually on the top. Frustrated, embarrassed and ashamed of my reality, I sought help from hair loss professionals. I saw a dermatologist who took a chunk of my scalp to diagnose my issue. I was hopeful, and then quickly disappointed. I was prescribed a topical ointment that made my scalp itch and peel, so I discontinued use. I wasn't giving up that easy, though. I visited a couple Hair Club for Men providers, only to be told I didn't have enough hair in the back of my head to cover what I'd lost.

In tears, feeling defeated, I gathered my things, went home, and sobbed. Thinking about it now, it seems very vain of me to fixate on something as simple as hair. It was bigger than that for me at the time. I couldn't shake the images of what it meant to be a beautiful woman. My hair became my identity. It consumed me. It governed my life. It dictated when and how to exercise. It required significant time and financial resources.

Because I needed to maintain a mask of beauty, I went on another pursuit. My pursuit led me to an amazing hair stylist whose hands were blessed by God Himself. She could work miracles and wonders with hair weaves and wigs. She was a genius. We experimented with different styles, colors, lengths and textures. She worked magic on my head for many years. We'd often be in the hair salon alone while she did my hair, because I didn't want anyone to see my reality. I'd often cry as she removed my weave, revealing a completely bald crown.

One day I posed a soul-shifting question to my miracle worker. At this point I'd grown tired of not being able to exercise like I wanted to, for fear of messing up my mask (my hair). I'd grown tired of not being able to ride roller coasters for fear of my weave flipping up and exposing my secret. I wanted to enjoy the sensation of my husband running his fingers through my hair without being paranoid that he'd feel the tracks. I was tired of spending hours in the hair salon crafting a masterpiece that masked me. Not to mention the amount of money I spent chasing after this elusive image of beauty. I was tired. I asked her jokingly, but seriously, "What if we just cut it all off?"

I'll never forget her reply. She said, "You'll be beautiful. But you have to know that. You'll do it when you're ready." I'd always think: what would my family think? What would happen with my job? What if I have huge dents and a funny-shaped head? This was our conversation for about four years. "You'll do it when you're ready."

I Choose Freedom

It was a typical Friday night. I was preparing to get my weave done the next morning. Planning to spend much of my Saturday in the salon.

As I was removing my weave, something hit me like a ton of bricks. I can't even begin to tell you what came over me, except it was the feeling of being done. Done with hiding my reality that I couldn't grow hair anymore. Done with caring about what other people thought of me. Done with being uncomfortable in my skin to make everyone else comfortable with how I looked. Done with not living because of what grows, or does not grow, out of the top of my head. DONE!

I called my stylist and said, "I'm done. I'm not applying another weave. We're shaving it off tomorrow. I'm not bringing in any hair, just in case I chicken out." I had to be all in.

She asked me if I was sure. At that moment, I couldn't have been more sure.

Typically, when I visit the salon it's empty. It's usually just me and my super stylist. On this particular Saturday the salon was PACKED. No chair was empty. And I had chosen this day to be bold. No turning back now.

I sat in her chair. She asked, "Are you ready?" I replied, "Let's do it." She pulled off my scarf, exposing my male balding hair pattern. She pulled out the clippers.

We both took a deep breath, and she started shaving. Shaving the weight I'd carried since I was 10 years old. Shaving my preconceived notions about beauty. Shaving to reveal the core of me. I Am Not My Hair.

As she shaved, we both cried. We cried tears of joy, in celebration of true liberty. I was free! I was a lover of me. Unapologetically me.

I am free! The other women in the salon were in awe. Their mouths literally dropped open at the sight of my completely bald head. No buzz or peach fuzz. Completely bald.

I gathered my things, gave my regards to my stylist for the many years spent together on this journey, and walked out of the salon liberated. I received so many compliments from men and women about my look and bravery. In the past, approval would have been so important to me; but something had happened. I didn't need it then nor in the days to follow. I wore freedom. When I think about it, people were not responding to what I looked like on the outside. They were responding to the work I'd done inside.

On this self-discovery journey I learned that beauty is an inside job. Beauty is the work we choose to do inside that then permeates out for the world to experience. I chose to redefine beauty. I wore confidence; the confidence that didn't know me when I was 10 years old... Heck, even 30 years old. I was confident living in my truth, my reality, and didn't apologize for it. *This is me, and I'm more than my hair.*

When it was time to face my family, I wasn't prepared for what I would experience. Up to this point, I'd told myself that I am more than just my hair and losing it doesn't compromise the essence of me. I'd believed that in my soul.

My look wasn't welcomed. I didn't realize that altering my look would result in not being spoken to for several weeks. Somehow, the choice I made was perceived as an affront. I had to reassure a couple of my family members that this had nothing to do with them and everything to do with me. I grew up in the church. The Bible talks about a woman's hair being her crown and glory. Because I didn't have mine anymore, somehow, I was perceived as having lost my religion, my mind, or both. Needless to say, there were members of my family who didn't approve. You know what? That was okay with me.

Living Out Loud

When I broke free of the bondage that was my hair, that's when I began living. That's when I took my first breath. I embodied courage and exuded confidence in myself. I'd finally showed up. New doors opened for me that I'd never imagined. I received an awesome promotion on my job. I started a new management consulting firm called Legacy Blueprint, LLC (look us up).

Fast forward a year. I was at a crossroad. I had to choose between staying with a company that I really enjoyed or quit to take a chance on my dream. People thought I was crazy to entertain the idea of quitting a stable, well-paying job with great benefits to pursue a business full-time with only two intermittent clients.

After much prayer and many sleepless nights, I decided to take a leap of faith. I resigned from my full-time job and pursued growing my business. How ironic: earlier in my life I had been pursuing things that I thought would fulfill me, only to be disappointed because "things" are temporary. Now my pursuits are living my best life and stretching myself to see what I'm really made of.

How has the journey been? My business is doing really well. I haven't been tempted to pick up a weave or wig to mask ME. Early on I considered having another biopsy to see if there's anything that can be done about my hair follicles. Then I had a little talk with myself, and it went a little something like this: "Self, we all good." I haven't looked back.

Early on I posed a question: "Who Am I?" You took a little walk with me as I shared my journey to arrive at the answer. Who Am I? I am courageous, stubborn, a lover of people. I am a trail blazer (I go first), intrinsically confident, particular, and empathetic. I am passionate, selfless and thoughtful. What I Am Not? I Am Not My Hair!

The Blueprint

What is your "I Am" and what's your "I Am Not?" We all hang on to the things that we think define who we are… to the point that it stunts our growth and ability to flourish. It robs us of living life out loud. It hinders the world from experiencing our true authentic self.

Let's get real for a moment. What would happen if we lost the very thing that we felt made us who we are? Something like our marital status, cars, homes, parental status, career, our health, or something as simple as wearing make-up? For me, it was my hair. How can we, or will we, pick up the pieces and continue thriving in life? It begins with getting to know who you are at your core; the essence of your being. A quote I love by Henry Stanley Haskins says, "What lies before us and what lies behind us are tiny matters compared to what lies within us." This quote articulates perfectly how the power that lies within propels us to be victorious even when life challenges us.

When I reflect on my journey of loving me inside out, I realize I unconsciously created a blueprint that helped me identify, understand, embrace and live in my "I Am." It took nearly forty years for me to get clear about who I am and embrace the unique contributions I've been created to make in this world.

How did I do it? I'm glad you asked. These steps will seem simple and basic to some of you. I've learned in many cases that making changes in life only requires simple and basic steps. My prayer is that they serve as a guide for you, too.

Let Go of Attachments

How do you let go of something or someone that once served a purpose but is now stifling your growth? The first question needs to be, how do you know if your growth is being stifled? Think about what you're attempting to accomplish. How does the individual or thing support or hinder you from getting there? For example, let's say your goal is to lose weight, but you won't exercise because you don't want to mess up your hair. Your hair is an attachment that is hindering you from achieving your goal. Now, I'm not saying cut it off. I am saying, get to the root of why your hair matters more than your goal. Recalibrate your mental model about the attachment. Maybe it's about choosing a different hairstyle until you achieve the goal.

How about people attachments? You know the ones. They attach themselves to you like that sea urchin in the aquarium that suctions itself to the glass wall. No matter what you do, it's hard to shake them. It starts to feel normal, and before you know it, they've drained you to the point that you have nothing left to invest in yourself. You're trying to catapult to your next level, but they are weighing you down. We've all heard the saying, "Where you're going in the next chapter of your life, not everyone is equipped, ready or meant to join you." The relationship or thing may have been suitable for a season. If you find that each time you take a leap towards your future you are pulled back, assess your attachments and govern yourself accordingly.

Assemble an Accountability Circle

A circle is something that is continuous with no breaks. It functions as a way to link and sometimes contain. A circle represents a sacred space. We've seen many graphics that depict the dynamic of circles; overlapping, concentric, inner and outer.

Let's talk about our inner circle. Who is a part of your most sacred space? Whom can you call when you've accomplished a huge goal, and they are just as excited, if not more excited, than you about your achievement? Whom do you call when you're having the worst day, month or year, to cry with you, encourage you, and pray with you? Who will tell you what you need to hear, not what you want to hear?

Having an effective accountability circle helps to keep us connected and focused on what we're striving to achieve and become. The selection of your accountability circle is crucial. There may be people whom you've known for a very long time that you may attempt to include in your circle by default. There is no default clause in this selection process. It's important to be deliberate, objective and picky. Before we talk about the characteristics one must embody in order to be invited to be a part of your accountability circle, let's talk about how you prepare yourself to be in the center of it.

- Know where you're heading. If you don't have a sense of your direction, you run the risk of making a poor selection.

- Tap the shoulder of people who are where you hope to be: people who have been there, done that, and don't mind sharing their keys to success.

- Develop an appetite to be told the truth.

Consider the following characteristics when making your selection. There may be other criteria that are important to you. Individuals must:

1. Exude confidence and be comfortable in their own skin. Your circle

should represent people who believe there's room in this world for everyone's gifts and talents and are genuinely excited about your accomplishments.

2. Have a track record of success and be open to sharing their wisdom.

3. Embody a spirit of discernment. There will be times when you'll get frustrated. A good accountability partner knows how long to allow you to vent and feel sorry for yourself before they challenge you to move to action. They'll say things like, "Get it together;" "You got this;" "You've cried long enough about this. I got your back. Let's make moves."

4. Have a sense of humor. This is definitely helpful for me but may not be necessary for you. A great leader I know always says, "If you don't laugh, you'll cry." I often find myself looking at the positive side of tough situations. Laughter has gotten me through many heartaches. The individuals in my circle possess a healthy sense of humor.

5. Be trustworthy and able to keep your business out of the streets. Enough said.

Discover Your Purpose

As a consultant I do a lot of executive coaching. One of the ways I begin to understand who my client is, as a person and as a leader, is to have them complete a variety of assessments. I decided to do the same for myself. Over the years I have completed a number of valid assessments that have all painted a vivid picture of my preferences, style, talents, etc. The revelations from the assessments, from my spirituality, from self-reflection, and from the support of my accountability circle have given me clarity about my purpose.

My purpose is to help people and organizations maximize their fullest potential, even when they don't see it. Realizing this purpose myself was a little tricky. I first had to get clear about my own potential and how to discover it. When I let go of what others thought of me and I embraced who I was, inside and out, I was ready to step into my purpose. It was then that doors opened for me.

If you're still in the process of discovering your purpose, ask yourself a few questions: What am I passionate about? What do I feel called to? What do people count on me for? What am I willing to make a sacrifice for? What career choice do I love so much that I could do it for free (not that you would, because you've gotta make a living)? The answers to these questions do not arrive overnight. Spend the next 30-60 days reflecting on the questions, and your direction will become clear. If you're able, invest in a career or life coach. A good coach is objective and knows the right questions to ask to help you hone in on what makes your heart sing. When you discover your purpose, don't be afraid to pursue opportunities that align with it. Your purpose was birthed in you on purpose. Invest in it, protect it and let others experience it.

Develop 100% Self-Belief (Yes, You're the Bomb)

If you don't believe in yourself, who will? Part of thriving in life is setting your eyes on the seemingly impossible. We will miss 100% of the shots we don't take. Possible becomes impossible when we don't have the courage to get in the game. There will be people watching on the sidelines trying to convince you that what you're hoping to achieve is not possible. You know what you're made of; and if you don't, you discover it by venturing out into the deep.

As I'm writing this section one of my favorite songs starts to play. It's a praise and worship song called, "I Am What You See" by William Murphy. Perfect timing. The lyrics go a little something like this:

> "Help me to see me. The way You see me. Sometimes I see pain, Lord. But You see victory. I see where I am, Lord. You see where I shall be. Open my eyes, help me believe I am what You see. You see me victorious. You see me faithful. You see me believing that You are able. You see me rejoicing 'cause I have survived. Open my eyes, help me believe I am what You see."

My spirituality is a huge part of who I am. This song articulates beautifully how I've been able to develop 100% belief in myself. How God sees me fuels my belief in myself. I pursue my dreams relentlessly because He sees me successful, so that's exactly what I'll be.

I encourage you to identify what motivates you to take chances and move to action. If you find yourself stuck and unable to move towards what you want, ask yourself, "If success was guaranteed, what bold steps would I take to move me towards my goals?" It starts with one bold step. The more you see success as a result of your actions, the more confidence you'll have in developing 100% belief in yourself. Self-belief doesn't mean we won't second guess ourselves or that we won't be fearful. Fear is a part of it. Use it to propel you, not paralyze you.

Be Unapologetically YOU

There is only one you. Many will try to duplicate, replicate, or perpetrate and want to be like you, but there's only one you. You do you better than anyone else could. You are fearfully and wonderfully made, and you have a unique purpose in this world.

What does it mean to be unapologetic? It is defined as not expressing regret. In other words, don't regret being you. I think it's important to share a caveat. Being unapologetic doesn't mean being rude, or saying hurtful things and justifying it by saying, "Well, this is who I am." So, let's take an appreciative approach to thinking about this. When you show up at a social gathering or a family event, or attend meetings in a professional setting, which YOU are you introducing? The you that you think people want to see, or the authentic, best version of you? When you show up, know that you have the power to disrupt, interrupt and change the atmosphere in a positive way, because of the essence of you. You are the answer. Acknowledge, own and be proud of what makes you different.

When you are in various settings and you find yourself debating whether to contribute a perspective, ask yourself this:

- What's at stake if I don't speak up?

- Considering my talents and gifts, what can I do or say in this moment to add value to the conversation or experience?

Try not to overthink it, wondering what people might say or think. I invite you to stand up tall in what makes you awesome. Don't apologize for it. No apology is needed for being the best version of you. If others have an issue with your greatness, that's their issue, not yours. Help them discover their own greatness by living in yours. Model the way.

Pay It Forward

The journey for me to discover and live in my "I Am" wasn't a short nor easy one. When I finally got it, my life changed. Imagine what our world would be like if we each reached back to support someone else who is on their own self-discovery journey. They may get there faster with your encouragement and transparency.

In particular, I think about our children, who are bombarded everyday with false images of what beauty, success and self-worth look like. It breaks my heart to see our young people mimic what they see on social media in an effort to be accepted, liked or popular. This infiltration of thought begins when we don't know our value and can't articulate who we are. I believe we have a responsibility to disrupt the epidemic.

I'd like to extend an invitation to you to lock arms with me and commit to supporting our young people in discovering their "I Am." Their lives and our futures depend on it. This can be done in a variety of different ways. For me it was becoming a parent mentor for a local not-for-profit organization. It could be as simple as giving a compliment that sends a message to a youth that who they are is enough. Or it could be as elaborate as hosting a seminar where the focus is on helping our youth discover their greatness. Whatever the gesture, if each of us commits to paying it forward, we can make a difference in the lives of this generation and the generations to follow.

During the process of writing my story, I have been going through a very difficult divorce. Severing a relationship that has spanned over half my life is one of the most difficult life experiences I've had to endure. I am thankful for having gone through a journey of self-discovery years prior to understand who I am, because without it I would have lost me in this process. My marriage was my life and losing it has left a scar that I'm not sure will ever completely heal. What I do know is that I need to stay connected to who I am.

The Blueprint that I shared with you helped me years ago and is still helping me today. No matter how trivial or catastrophic your situation is, get clear about who you are. When you ground yourself in that epiphany, it doesn't matter how hard the wind blows or how violently the earth shakes; you'll be able to live your life with the assurance that you'll be just fine. It won't always be easy, but you will be victorious.

Namaste
(from my heart to yours)

Laticia Thompson

"If your dreams don't scare you then they aren't big enough." Laticia (Tish) Thompson, born and raised in Joliet, IL, embodies this sentiment. For much of her life she has taken deliberate steps to challenge the status quo, test her limits, and step into fear vs. run away from it. Attending high school graduation four months pregnant motivated Tish to defy the stereotypes that are associated with being a teenage mom. She made it her mission to build a comfortable life for her family and knew that a college education was the key. In addition to her business degree, she holds a Master of Science degree in Management and Organizational Behavior with concentrations in Human Resources and Organizational Development. Tish is currently pursuing her doctorate degree in Business Psychology.

Stepping outside of her comfort zone, Tish founded a management consulting firm called Legacy Blueprint, LLC. The firm was birthed to help organizations and individuals maximize their fullest potential. Legacy Blueprint, LLC partners with organizations to provide the blueprint for strategy cultivation and execution, staff and leadership development, executive coaching and employee engagement support. Because of the success of her firm she was faced with having to make one of the toughest decisions in her career: play it safe and remain in her steady, well-paying job, or step out on faith and pursue her dream of growing her business. She stepped out on faith and hasn't looked back.

Tish is described by many as a dedicated mom of four, a trailblazer, an infectious motivational speaker and facilitator, a passionate entrepreneur, and a five time marathon finisher. Tish is passionate about giving back to the community and will soon be launching a not-for-profit organization for pregnant teens. Are her dreams big enough? Absolutely!! She will tell you she's terrified... in a good way!

Laticia Thompson
Legacy Blueprint, LLC
1147 Brook Forest Avenue, #118
Shorewood, IL 60404
815-919-4940
lthompson@legacy-blueprint.com
www.legacy-blueprint.com

Valerie Mrak

Journey to Peace

When you give in to anger, you lose your intelligence.
—His Holiness the Dalai Lama

It was a simple yet elegant, incense-filled office in Dharamsala, India. As I offered the white ceremonial scarf to His Holiness the Dalai Lama in the traditional greeting, I felt a combination of excitement and wonder. Little did I know that in a few minutes, our video interview with the exiled Tibetan spiritual leader would turn my world upside down and change the trajectory of my life.

Outwardly Successful

My life looked like an adventure. I was a successful, independent video producer who got to interview fascinating people like His Holiness the Dalai Lama, Blackfoot medicine women and best-selling authors. I had won awards for my work, been a founding member and leader of a national trade organization, and in 1995 was named one of *Today's Chicago Woman's 100 Women to Watch*. But underneath, I was angry. It was not a momentary moody response to something that wasn't going my way. It was a deep, gut-level anger that was an integral part of me.

My rage was eating at my marriage and my relationship with my step-daughter. I spent more and more time working and sleeping in my studio, which was located 60 miles from my home. My business relationships were difficult. I felt that I was being taken advantage of by one colleague and being treated unfairly by another. I got fired by a client. A friendship of over 20 years was fading. My health was not the best. I had gained 50 pounds and was depressed most of the time.

Anger was a paralyzing, alienating, tumultuous, seething, emotional undercurrent that I worked ceaselessly to keep in check. Until I couldn't.

Ka-pow!

In that interview with the Dalai Lama, we asked him what he meant when he said in his Nobel Peace Prize acceptance speech that he would like for Tibet to be set aside as a Zone of Peace. As Westerners, we expected something bureaucratic, like a building, or a commission, or a council. Instead, he said, "It would be a place of peace toward animals, a place of peace toward the environment, a place of peace toward fellow man. But that is all external peace, of course. Before you can have external peace, you must have a zone of peace in your heart."

That statement hit me like a thunderbolt. What was that? It certainly wasn't something I had! How do you get it? What did that mean for me as a non-Buddhist, white, American, mid-western woman who came of age in the early 1970s amid Vietnam protests, civil rights, women's rights, and the sexual revolution?

Seeking Answers

As a documentary filmmaker, I ask questions. I began to conduct research by asking people in elevators, strangers at street corners, friends, colleagues — pretty much everybody I met in the course of my day: "What is peace to you? Who are your peace role models?" I learned that:

- People fumble when they try to define peace,; even when they describe themselves as being at peace.

- Our role models for peace are more often cultural icons rather than people with whom they've actually interacted (Martin Luther King, Mother Theresa, Mahatma Gandhi, for instance).

- Many people don't believe they have much agency over peace between themselves and others (think of the current divide in conversations in the political arena, even between people who are otherwise loving).

I also researched peace memorials around the world. I discovered that the vast majority of them are either monuments to dead soldiers or tributes to great battle strategists. They teach us nothing about incorporating peace into our actual lives—our homes, workplaces, schools, and communities.

I was granted another interview with the Dalai Lama, specifically to explore peace. His answer to my role model question surprised me. I expected him to say his Buddhist teachers. Instead, he said, "My mother."

Aha?

I started seeking *living* role models. I knew I didn't want people whose position I couldn't relate to—like leaders who were heads of state or who held lofty positions to which I could never aspire. With the exception of the Dalai Lama, of course!

I discovered a group of Nobel Peace Prize winners who were average citizens at the time they were given the award—a secretary and a waitress from Northern Ireland, an attorney from Iran, a homemaker from Burma (now Myanmar), and a professor from Argentina. Each had been living in an area of ongoing conflict and had experienced personal tragedy in that conflict: losing family, being imprisoned, being stripped of their social and economic status, or being tortured. Yet they stood up for peace, and their actions changed or affected the course of the conflict. They each agreed to an interview, and a picture began to emerge of just what peace might be.

At a peace event in Chicago, I met a man who was a former gang leader and former violent offender. After serving many years in prison, he had returned to his Chicago neighborhood intent on mitigating the kind of violence he had perpetrated as a youth. I was surprised and fascinated that this man who had succumbed to devastating anger that led to the worst kind of violence had created peace within himself and was now reaching out to youth. What he shared with me mirrored much of what the Nobel Laureates shared about creating peace.

The operative word here is creating. Peace is a created act. We choose to create peace, moment by moment. With apologies to dictionary makers and grammar-pundits everywhere, think of peace as a verb—not as a noun or an adjective.

Mairead Corrigan Maguire from Northern Ireland, one of the Nobel Laureates I interviewed, said,

> *"All of us must make our own pilgrimage to peace. This pilgrimage is unique. It must go in two directions. One road leads inward to the depths of our being; the other road leads outward to our fellow human beings and the universe. For many, the inner road is less known and less traveled."*

The Inner Road

I knew I had inner work to do.

I coupled my conversations about peace with a dive into ontology, which is a philosophical inquiry into the nature of being. What I learned was brilliant. It was one of those things that's easy to understand, yet takes a bit of work to master.

Self-doubt, fear and anger started quite early in my life. I was the second of five children, the second daughter, with three younger brothers following. When I was five years old, my first younger brother was born, and he was the first son in our Eastern European family. I felt as if I went from the pampered youngest to persona non grata in an instant. You fellow middle children will know what I mean.

I believed I was invisible, unheard, and insignificant.

When I was nine years old, I had an extensive, distressing skin aberration. This was just at the beginning of allergy science, and I was tested with little bits of allergen substances up and down both arms. As a result, they swelled up horribly, making me resemble the Michelin Man!

I was diagnosed as allergic to pretty much everything: grass, weeds, trees, mold, dust, mildew, gluten, dairy, citrus, legumes, mushrooms, and pork. Every morning, skin that wasn't covered with clothing was coated in thick zinc oxide and wrapped up to keep it from being exposed to the environment. Each school day for my *entire* third grade year, I toted the same lunch—a cold hamburger patty and a banana. There were no such things as gluten- or dairy-free alternatives at that time. I coveted my classmates' mac and cheese and their peanut butter sandwiches on Wonder bread.

The experience—that I would carry with me for decades—left me feeling damaged, deprived, and alone.

Invisible, unheard, and insignificant, plus damaged, deprived, and alone. Who wouldn't be angry?

What I learned through ontology is that stuff happens: *When I was five years old, my brother was born.* Immediately, we create an interpretation of what happened: *I'm not good enough, because I'm a girl. Between my brilliant and beautiful older sister and my bratty younger brothers, nobody even cares about me. I don't count!*

Persistence

Now I don't want to have you think I was having a pity party from the time I was 5 years old…well, I sort of was.

However, being invisible, unheard, and insignificant, plus damaged, deprived, and alone also helped me develop some strengths. One of those strengths was persistence. I was determined to get what I wanted. And because I was invisible, I could be secretive about it. This sometimes worked out incredibly well, and sometimes it got me in trouble.

For instance, my first-grade classmates and I were munching on our lunches. I informed my teacher that the salty potato chips we were served were burning my chapped lips and that I didn't want them. She demanded that I eat them or I couldn't go out to recess. I pleaded my case again. She insisted and walked away. I did what I thought was clever and resourceful: I threw the chips under the table and blithely went out to play. When we went back in to the classroom, my teacher was waiting for me with a wooden paddle in hand, and I was publicly humiliated and punished for my disobedience.

What I took from that experience is that adults could not to be relied on. I would need to be much more clever—as in secretive—in the future to get what I wanted.

Another example of my "cleverness": Within a few months of starting college at the age of seventeen, I fell in love with a young man. By the middle of the second semester, I was struggling in school. During that summer, I moved in with my boyfriend and did not return to the dorm in the fall. My parents knew nothing of my having moved out of the dorm, my struggling in school, nor of the relationship. When they found out, they were so furious that they disowned me. Completely. No college funding. No family holidays. No contact with them or my siblings. And my boyfriend and I soon broke up. I was left on my own.

There was a serious recession in 1973. I could not find work. Because I was still enrolled at the university, even though I had quit going to classes, I was considered "voluntarily poor" and could not get any kind of public assistance. I had no money, no prospects, no one to lean on, and no food. Luckily, before having been disowned, I had paid some months ahead for a one-room, dilapidated apartment. With my last bit of cash, I bought a book on foraging wild plants and learned to harvest greens from the vacant lots around my college town. It was the one and only time period I ever shoplifted. I felt so guilty that I only did it a couple of times. Ironically, I chose honesty over being a sneak-thief. I also learned that perfectly good food got thrown away behind grocery stores and fast food places at specific times every day. Between foraging and dumpster diving, I was able to survive for many months.

Eventually, I was able to piece together three part-time jobs and get back into college. With the championing of my compassionate and insistent sister, a future labor lawyer, I was slowly accepted back into the family. On both sides, as you can imagine, there was a lot of mending to do.

I learned from this experience that I'm resilient and tenacious, and I learned how important it is to speak up. This is where my journey started as a documentary filmmaker, intent on providing an opportunity for myself and others to have our voices heard—out loud.

Persistence Pays Off

I am often asked how I get to interview the people that I do. I think it's because I am dedicated to telling stories that teach us something about ourselves. And when I learned to use my voice in service to that, people began to say yes. Of course, sometimes the yes came only after my asking multiple times. And sometimes I had to settle for a no. Ultimately, the people I have interviewed, from the Blackfoot women and the former gang leaders and the Nobel Prize winners and the "everyday" people, have had something they wanted to say, and they trusted that I would listen.

While I was doing my research on peace, I began thinking that it could turn into a documentary. All of those people I was talking to every day, asking about peace definitions and role models, wanted me to share what I was learning with them.

Facing Demons

I took on bold actions in my life, despite my inner feelings.

Remember that dive into ontology that I mentioned? We were instructed to write down three assessments about ourselves—things we held as true. I wrote these three items down:

- I have everyone fooled—I'm not very smart.
- I'm really not creative.
- I'm dull and boring.

My whole life, I'd been creating accomplishments, desperately running ahead of these assessments about myself. I was exhausted!

Then we were instructed to share with the person next to us. The person next to me shared something like: I'm very capable, intuitive and compassionate. *What?!* It didn't even occur to me that a self-assessment could include anything positive.

We were then instructed to prove these assessments by stating facts about ourselves. Well, I couldn't prove anything. I had a college degree. People sought out my advice. I had a body of award-winning work. I was involved in and a leader of trade organizations. What an eye-opener!

But that lesson seemed to go no further than myself. Some months later, I accepted some coaching around my troubled relationship with my husband, Michael. I declared that the relationship wasn't working because he was uneducated, uncreative, and uninvolved. Does that sound familiar? Those were just different words for my own bankrupt self-assessment months earlier!

I was asked if I could give up those beliefs, and I agreed. After all, I had done it for myself. And then I had nothing. Nothing at all. I didn't know who he was. I didn't know who I was in relationship to him. I didn't know who we were together. I began to flop-sweat, sob hysterically, and shake like a leaf. This went on for hours. I thought I would dehydrate.

I appealed to my coach, "Please help me. I need some other assessments to hang on to!" He laughed and said, "That's not how it works." It was up to me to explore our relationship and my husband newly, to be open and curious.

Once I settled into a compromise with the unknown, I called Michael and told him what I had experienced. He was quiet for a few minutes and then asked, "Does that mean you're going to be more open with me?" I was. I am. I got a whole new view of my husband. I discovered that Michael is kind. He's industrious, and he's my biggest supporter.

Taking Responsibility

I had been so used to doing things my way and working under the radar, to avoid the scrutiny of anyone in authority, that it was a major move toward becoming a responsible adult the first time I took accountability for messing up. I'm a bit embarrassed to admit that I was well into my thirties.

It was late. There was a tight deadline and I was supervising an edit for my client's client through the long night. My client trusted me with his vision. But for some reason, I went rogue. I made choices for how to approach telling the story that were decidedly counter to his thinking.

He came in the next morning to review the video and prepare for his client meeting. To his shock and consternation, what was laid out for him was not the approach he had promised the client. He was furious.

I quickly thought that maybe I could plead misunderstanding or defend my vision as the better one—or blame the editor. I freely considered the shameless blaming of anyone or anything else.

Instead, I took a deep breath. I took responsibility. I apologized. I offered to fix the edit at my own hefty expense. I withstood my client's wrath, distress, and sense of having been betrayed. I fixed the edit after he re-negotiated the deadline with his client, and I knew I would never be working with my favorite client again.

I was wrong. Taking accountability for my actions actually built a sense of trust between us. We went on to work with each other for several more years, even becoming officemates, sharing work for each other's clients and continuing our creative partnership.

I still have that life-time, knee-jerk desire to deflect responsibility. Now, however, when I mess up, I breathe deeply, accept accountability, and clean up whatever there is to clean up.

Shut Up and Listen

One way of taking responsibility, however counter-intuitive, is to just listen. The greatest gift you can give someone is to listen to them. All people want to feel like they've been heard. As a child who felt insignificant, learning to sit quietly was a gift I developed early. Once when I was working with a client, I was asked to engage with a particular graphic designer. Every other producer who had ever worked with her warned me about how unpleasant it was to work with her. She complained loudly and often.

When I met her, she launched into a series of complaints that lasted—no kidding—over two hours. I didn't say much. I nodded, mmm-hmm'd, and occasionally interjected a question, and then she was off to her kvetching once again. When we finally got to the project at hand that night, which had a tight turn-around, she not only finished the work brilliantly and early, she made changes for me with little grumbling.

It was the beginning of a delightful partnership for us, simply because I had been willing to listen. Everyone else she'd worked with had shut her down. I allowed her to open up.

Leap!

Many things I've accomplished have come from taking a leap of faith: every documentary film I ever made, starting my own video production business, speaking to audiences about creating peace, choosing trust.

Every time I've made that leap, I've learned something precious that I will use for the rest of my life.

Take a bicycle ride, for instance. I'm no athlete and have never been one. I trained for a 500-mile, 6-day AIDS charity ride for months and still was a very slow rider. I was on my bike from sunrise to sunset to be able to make 70-100 miles each day.

And then it was Hill Day. I had missed hill training due to an injury. I was terrified. The first hill was on an old railroad bed. The 7-mile-long grade was so gradual, it wasn't even detectable. Yet it got harder and harder to pedal. I was distraught, crying at the effort it took this early in the morning. I pulled off to the side to calm myself when another rider joined me. He told me that there was no shame in finding the ride to be difficult. He had sagged into camp every day for the first few years he did the ride. I asked him why he kept doing it if it was so hard. He replied, "Because my son has AIDS. He promises to live another year, and I do this ride another year." Fresh tears got me on the bike again, and I rode for him and his son.

The next hill I encountered rose like a monolith in front of me. However, I was determined. I began to pedal as fast as I could, and then I hit the grade. It was like hitting a wall. I stood on the pedals, willing them to go around fast enough to keep the bike upright. I knew I wouldn't make it up. Then from the top of the hill, two young athletic riders came running down to me. They put their hands on my back and jogged up the hill with me, taking some of the strain out of the climb.

The next hill I saw was some distance away. I geared up, pedaling faster and faster, determined to win this one all by myself. When I got to the tree that had looked like it was on top of the hill, I realized that the hill had been an optical illusion. I had engaged in all that hard work for nothing!

Finally, only 20 more miles to camp. One last hill rose up in the distance. It was daunting, but now I had mastered the technique and knew how to get up it. As I was gearing up, pedaling faster and faster, I saw a rider crying at the bottom. I thought I'd give her an encouraging "Almost there, Rider!" as I made my own way up, but kindness stopped me. I persuaded her back on her bike and rode just behind her while shouting words of encouragement. We got up that last hill together.

What I learned from Hill Day is that hills on a bicycle are a lot like those things you do while taking a leap in life. Sometimes, you keep going because someone has touched your heart. Sometimes, when things seem just too difficult, someone shows up to lighten the load. Sometimes, you can work really hard at something that wasn't a challenge at all. And sometimes, it's good to stop and help someone along their way.

The Outer Road

I never did make that documentary about peace. I discovered that my voice needed to be heard in another way. I now lead talks and workshops on Conflict to Possibility, sharing with people how they can utilize the insights I gained from being with the Nobel Peace Laureates and former gang leaders. People have had breakthroughs in their work relationships, have re-ignited lost friendships, and have renewed the spirit for connection between their organization and community. And one international traveler defused a particularly rancorous incident at a notoriously hostile airport using what she learned from my workshop.

Being persistent. Taking responsibility. Making bold leaps. Understanding that opinion is not truth. Listening to really hear someone. Being open and vulnerable. All of these led me to creating peace and new possibilities in my work and in my personal life—as a speaker, a coach, a business partner, a neighbor, a friend, a sister, a wife. I am grateful for the many extraordinary, courageous, and loving friends, family, and teachers along the way.

It is my belief that as we create peace in ourselves and in our relationships, that we are developing the ability to create peace in the world. Where and with whom will you create peace? Take the leap.

Valerie Mrak

Speaker • Coach • Storyteller • Filmmaker

Valerie is a visionary leader, inspiring workshop participants with new and engaging concepts. Her unique and laser-like skills in listening help them move from the impossible to the doable with ease.

She traveled the world exploring peace and interviewing Nobel Peace Laureates, including His Holiness the Dalai Lama. She also worked with former gang leaders and former violent offenders who were working for peace in their neighborhoods.

Valerie leads Conflict to Possibility workshops and trainings for businesses, community organizations and youth groups, as well as mastering effective communication skills. Her TEDx talk, Peace Inside/Out, can be viewed at https://you.be/NpHE2Q_QM6E.

She is a storyteller, leads story-telling workshops and tells original stories at public performances around the Chicago area. She has also been a storyteller with the National Park Service, relating traditional folk tales in addition to regional favorites.

Her Telly Award-winning documentary Shadow Over Tibet: Stories in Exile, a film about Tibetan immigrants in America and India, striving to maintain their religion and culture in exile aired nationally on PBS. It features a personal interview with the Dalai Lama and is narrated by Richard Gere.

She has produced videos for mitigation experts and defense attorneys that provided juries with a vital understanding of the early lives and environments of defendants being considered for the death penalty. Her work contributed to juries and judges choosing alternative sentences over death for her clients' cases.

Valerie served as media director for Youth Technology Corps, where she sparked a 5-year US-Mexico youth documentary exchange and she produced and directed a children's video on the environment.

She lives on the southern shore of Lake Michigan with her husband, Michael.

Valerie Mrak
Mrakulous Productions
773-255-1425
mrakulous1@gmail.com
www.mrakulous.com
www.ConflictToPossibility.com

Natalya Melnik

Never Give Up

Well hello there! So nice to meet you! My name is Natalya Melnik. I'm a mom of seven kiddos. I was born in Russia and moved to America in February 1993. My story is full of struggles, but also of victories and wins.

Coming to America was both a blessing and a challenge. When I lived in Russia, I vowed that someday I would have a whole loaf of bread to myself. I didn't always have food in my belly, so it was very exciting to be going to a place that had those resources available. Little did I know that other challenges awaited me.

To this day, I can vividly see the time I sat at my desk and cried with frustration, "I don't understand!" as my teacher handed me a book report I needed to write. I didn't just cry; I bawled my eyes out! Wanting to make friends but not understanding them, and vice versa, was very challenging. I vowed that wouldn't stop me. From not speaking or writing in English, I quickly mastered the language and won a spelling bee. I can still hear the teacher telling a classmate of mine, "How can you not know how to spell 'there' in the correct form when this girl whose first language isn't English can do it?" I felt bad for the student, but it gave me hope that I could achieve things if I wanted them badly enough. And so began my journey to something much greater, from making the Honor Roll, National Honor Society, and Phi Theta Kappa, to getting into a doctorate program to become a Doctor of Pharmacy. Now the real challenges began.

It's always been a dream of mine to be a pharmacist. It all began one day when my 12-year-old self was getting cinnamon and spearmint essential oils to make my own "spicy and good for your breath" toothpicks. Who remembers making those as a kid? Back in the day they were the coolest new thing! As I stood there in the pharmacy section, trying to pick out the flavors of the oils for my next creation, something dawned on me. So much medicine, so many bottles and pills... and the doctor that all the people came to, to ask for a recommendation for one ailment or another... I wanted to do that! I wanted to help people with their pain! I wanted people to feel better!

As the years went on, I got married, had three kiddos, and was accepted into an accelerated Doctor of Pharmacy program. Unfortunately, that dream career came to a halt when my 3-month-old son got sick with pneumonia and had to be hospitalized for a couple of weeks. I initially wanted to go back the following year, but quickly found out that I was expecting my fourth child. I made a career change to be a nurse, and the following year I got into a nursing program. But at around five months pregnant I went into labor and was put on bed rest. My nursing career came to a halt. Maybe it was a sign from heaven? Little did I know that a few short months later, when my son was born, he would almost die. Just before we were to go home, he spat up green stuff. I was lost. It was my fourth child and I'd never seen that before, especially with a newborn that was breastfed exclusively. A whirlwind of heartache, confusion, tears, and prayers followed, as the doctors did test after test to find out what was wrong with my son. Thank God, they finally found the problem and were able to perform the surgery he needed successfully. The rest of that year was filled with appointments, and he being sick pretty much all the time took a huge toll on me. I wanted to go back to school and finish my education! So, when my son felt better, I went back to the pursuit of my career.

I was debating nursing or being a dental hygienist, and picked the latter. As my new pursuit of this career began, my son, that was now a few months old, got pneumonia. I was angry with myself for putting him into daycare and now for having to deal with the same problems as my other son—or were they? I was devastated! "What's going on?" I asked myself. I had good grades and good intentions, but I kept having obstacles.

I left school to take my son to the hospital. While there, he stopped breathing and turned blue. I screamed! My world seemed to end! I cried for the nurse and watched in a blur as doctors and nurses and hospital staff ran to my son, trying to resuscitate him! Tears are streaming down my face as I relive that horrible moment. The pain is so raw. It's reaching to the core of my bones. I didn't know if my son would make it or if he was gone. The next few hours were excruciating. But by God's amazing mercy and grace, he survived! This crisis brought me to the decision that my kids came first, and that school was out of the equation.

I began searching for income opportunities where I could work from home and support my family. One direct sales company, then another, then another... all ended up not bringing me the breakthrough I needed. Yes, I climbed the ranks and brought in some income, but none gave me financial freedom. Then I came across a company I thought would be the one; I would get that freedom. But the unthinkable happened.

Life threw the worst arrows at me. It didn't rain, it didn't pour... it deluged and hit me with the force of a tsunami! The world as I knew it... shattered. All my dreams and hopes fell apart. I was left empty, alone, homeless, depressed, anxious, and not wanting to live. I lost my entire family. Pregnant with my sixth child, homeless, without my kids and not knowing where they were. No husband. NO ONE. I was done. I felt numb. The way it all fell upon me, the false accusations, the rumors, the attacks, the judgements... I was broken. I looked for a way out of this life. Nothing seemed to be holding me here anymore. The pain I felt, I wouldn't wish it upon my worst enemy. NO ONE deserves to go through what I went through.

I lived like that for a few months. Then the threats for my unborn baby started coming in. I needed a place to live. Eventually I was able to get into a shelter—which was not easy at all—just a week before I gave birth. The obstacles I had to go through in order to get in were extremely frustrating and unfair, but I kept going. I had to. My unborn son needed to be taken care of.

And then, he was born.

For a few days' things seemed ok. But then I was hit again with incredible pain and unfairness! Where was justice? A fellow lady that was staying in the shelter said my son wasn't breathing. I was shocked! They started shaking my perfectly healthy newborn. I was disgusted! What were they doing!? It wasn't my first baby. I knew he was healthy. I had taken him to the doctors a few times just that week, for his appointments and my own.

At the emergency room they wanted to do a spinal tap on my perfectly healthy baby! I asked them why they thought it was necessary; my son wasn't showing any signs of distress, he looked and acted perfectly fine, and was breathing without any issues at all. I knew if I didn't look out for and advocate for my son, no one would. They did all kinds of tests on him, only to say, "Your son is perfectly healthy and there's nothing wrong with him." Because I was living in the shelter, I wasn't allowed to stay with my son overnight. I was devastated. He was only about a week old. I was nursing. I had to go back and pump.

The next day I was going to go back to the hospital, but was told not to come: my son was now in foster care. Oh my God, WHY??? WHY??? I cried like never before. I hadn't done anything wrong. I did everything I possibly could to ensure he and all my kids had everything they needed, and that they were taken care of and loved unconditionally. But because someone deemed it their right, my family was torn apart. I lost my milk supply because of the stress. I was forced to go to a Crisis Center when they took my baby away, to prove yet again that I was ok. They ran tests and treatments, assigned parenting classes... you name it, I did it. I did it all to prove to them that I was a fit parent in their eyes. Parenting classes? Really? I could teach those. But I went anyway. I was always on the go. I did everything above and beyond to prove them wrong. I prayed all the time. That was my only anchor, my only way to be able to get through the horror I was living. The story of Job comes to mind, how he lost everything and still stayed faithful. I was stolen from and lied about, and rumors were spread about me. But I kept going. I didn't give up. I lived one day at a time, one minute at a time. I dedicated every possible moment to reading the Bible and praying for a miracle. I begged God to step up for me and my family.

The next blow came: I was told my kids were being put up for adoption. I had no say. I was in shock. How could this be happening? I still couldn't fathom why they would take kids away from a good home and put them through so much stress. I felt worthless, like unwanted garbage that needed to be thrown out and completely wiped from the earth. During this whole process, I felt like a failure. Like I was never good enough, unwanted, unloved. Like I was the ugliest and least capable person on the entire planet. That I could never amount to anything. I believed those lies. I wanted to die. But I kept pushing, even though everything in me screamed to give up. I said, "Just for today, just one more time, keep pushing." And I did. I kept fighting. I told myself, I will never give up on my kids! I fought with every cell in my body.

Eventually I got my youngest son back. I went back to school, and while pregnant with my seventh child, finished at the top of my class as a medical interpreter. I got my house back. Got all my kids back. Bought a new house. And then I started my own online business. I tried doing parties, but people in this day and age have gotten so sick of them, many have straight out told me that they're "out-partied." Red flags started to appear, and I was looking for a way out.

Here begins the story of my career path. When my seventh child was born, my skin started wreaking havoc on me. I've always struggled with acne, since I was a teenager, and it would come and go. But after giving birth to my seventh child my acne flared up and became severe. I got deeply pitted, purple acne scars. My whole face hurt! My skin texture became rough like sand paper, and nothing was helping me. I tried everything under the sun, from cheap store brands to luxurious expensive brands to doctor's prescriptions. Nothing helped. I would hide from people. I would avoid social gatherings and not swim in public, and I even hid from my mailman when he would ring the doorbell. I was miserable. I was praying so hard for a solution. I was actually praying for two things: for good skin care that would heal my face, and a job that I could work from home. (There was no way I was going to put my kids in daycare or be separated from them again.)

As I was trying to leave my previous company, I came across a Facebook post about a brand-new skincare company that had just launched the previous month, in February 2018. The products had natural ingredients and were vegan, gluten free, cruelty free, and free from toxic chemicals. The post was intriguing, but I had almost lost all hope that something could work for my skin... and also, I was so sick of direct sales companies. But as I tried scrolling past, this thought crossed my mind out of nowhere: "Click on it." *Weird,* I thought. *I don't want to.* As I proceeded to try to scroll past, the thought came again: "Click on it." *Ok, now this is really strange,* I thought. Why am I getting this thought? I don't want to click on it. And as I put down my finger and was in the process of scrolling, the thought came at me so sternly—"CLICK ON IT!"—that I got chills all over my body! I knew it was God telling me to click on it. So, I gave it a try. And it has changed my life around COMPLETELY! Not only did I get the answer to my skin concerns, but also the biggest blessing: the career of my dreams!

I became one of the top leaders in the company and got to go to the exclusive all-paid leadership retreat! I became one of the select few ladies that got to be a part of the Advisory Board. And I got to be in a very exclusive photo shoot for the company. Wow! How did all that happen? It happened with lots of perseverance, consistency, and taking action. There are crucial steps I learned during all my trials and errors. They have finally given me the answers I've been looking for. And now, I want to share those tips with you.

Are you ready to be the next success story? Then you need to follow what I'm about to tell you to the T. These steps are crucial to the growth of your business today. They will teach you how to become a massive action taker, and take you from being someone "stuck" in your head to actually moving forward.

Tip Number 1

Start entering into things with the mindset that you just want to experience it, and that you want to learn and grow. This relieves you from the pressure of thinking everything needs to be perfect (oftentimes that thought can hold you back). If something scares you, switch your mindset to: "I'm just going to learn from it. I'm just going to do it and not really care how it comes out. If I fall on my face, fine; I'll get back up. I'm going to learn something from this experience." Any experience is a good experience because you're going to learn and grow from it.

Tip Number 2

Shift your thoughts from what could go wrong to what could go RIGHT! Focusing on the negative will only stop you from taking action. It is completely natural for our minds to look at the worst case scenario, but it is much more beneficial to train your mind to look at the best case scenario. It's all a matter of perspective. Stop thinking about everything that could go wrong and start thinking about all the lovely things that could go right.

Tip Number 3

Have more faith in yourself. If others can or have done what you want to do, then why can't you? Most highly successful people are not brilliant, or mentor members, or born with more advantages than you. How many successful people do you know of that started off incredibly poor? No skills. Learning disabilities. Right? They ALL had faith in themselves, and they backed that faith up with action.

Tip Number 4

Be ok with failure and be willing to take some calculated risks. If you're too afraid of failure you will not take these risks, right? What is the worst that could happen? You would have an experience. You would learn and grow: how bad is that? This is the mindset that makes many people feel absolutely fine about failure, and even embrace it.

Tip Number 5

Have a strategy for getting yourself out of a funk FAST. It happens to ALL of us. Your day is going along, and you just find yourself in that mental funk where you feel like you didn't get a sale, none of your conversations really led anywhere, you didn't move forward in your business today. We all have days like that. Or, here is another example. Something happens with a teammate, somebody says something that kind of rubs you the wrong way or hurts your feelings, and you find yourself in that funk. You find yourself going: "Oh my goodness, can I do this?" A bit of self-doubt starts to creep in. It happens to EVERYONE. You absolutely must have a strategy for getting yourself out of that funk, and quickly. Get off the computer/phone and go read a book (the Bible or something for your personal development), watch a motivational video on YouTube, pray, go help someone, exercise or do something physical. Change your mentality. Perceiving something as positive or negative is up to you. Ask yourself, "Why did I create this? Obviously, I'm meant to get something out of this. What am I meant to get out of it? What am I meant to learn? How am I going to use it to grow?" You can take anything that happens and change the way you look at it and make it a good thing.

Tip Number 6

Visualization. Stop looking at just today (if you're in that funk) and think about where you want to be six months from now, a year from now, five years from now. What will your life look like? Sometimes looking at the bigger picture makes what's happening that day more insignificant. You have to think bigger. Think past today.

Pick one activity that will make the most impact on your business today. It's usually that thing you've been avoiding. What is one income-producing or business-building activity you can do today to really push your business forward? Chances are, it involves having a lot of conversations. If you don't feel like your business is moving forward, stop working on something techy that's frustrating you, and build relationships. Set a goal for yourself and make it happen. Sometimes you won't go to bed until you get a sale or a sign up... But notice how this changes the vibration of the entire next day. You're now on fire and ready to conquer the world!

Tip Number 7

COMMIT. Commit to yourself and your future. Just make a decision and stick to it. Today might be the day you need to draw it in your mind and set it. You've got to make that decision to show up every single day. Not someday; not every second day; EVERY DAY. Building a business is an uphill climb in the beginning. If it's difficult for everyone, why should it be any different for you?

If you're in a car and you're going uphill, if you take your foot off the gas pedal you start to roll backwards. You're going to find yourself at the bottom of that hill, and how are you going to get back up? You need to hit the gas again to go back up. If you keep doing this back and forth action, it won't help you to get to the top of the hill. The ONLY WAY you're going to get to the top is to not take your foot off the gas pedal. Refuse to do that to yourself, and commit. Stop giving in to your excuses. If you're coming up with all kinds of reasons why you shouldn't do it, you are self-sabotaging and you will never create the success that you desire.

Tip Number 8

You need to get out of victim mode and into creator mode. Stop seeing yourself as a victim of your circumstances and start acting like the creator you are. Staying in victim mode is a choice; it's an excuse. Victim mode is going to keep you forever stuck and not able to move forward in creating the life that you want. You are a CREATOR. There are a lot of people (that you know) who have been able to create what you want. Why is that? It's a mindset. They don't see themselves as victims, and you can no longer do that either. You've got to know that the time is NOW. Stop procrastinating. Time is passing you by.

Intention is a wonderful thing… goals, dreams, beliefs; those are wonderful things. But if you're not backing those things up with ACTION, they're not going to happen for you. You do not lose by taking action; you can only lose by NOT taking action. Wishful thinking is not enough; if it were, the world would be full of billionaires, wouldn't it? Back up your dreams with action or you're going to have nothing. Words mean nothing; results do.

A year from now, do you want to be going: Oh my goodness, look at how I've created myself. Look at what I've created for my family. I did this in one year! Or, do you want to sit there and go: I'm no further ahead. I created no growth in my business. I'm in exactly the same place I was a year ago. Don't be in that position. You have FULL control over how fast you go, the amount of action you take, the amount of results you create. Right? So, exercise that. Use your power to create whatever you want.

I hope this inspires you to go out and start taking massive action. Think about where you want to be in a year. Think about being able to look at your family and say: I had no idea that I was going to be able to do that so fast and be so successful, but I did it! It feels pretty good when you can say that to people, and they see that happening year after year. Be that person, and make it happen!

Natalya Melnik

Natalya is the mother of seven beautiful children, who are her whole world. She loves Jesus and says, "By the Grace of God, I made it this far." She came to the USA as a refugee in 1993 and has come to call America her home. She loves cooking, baking, singing, and playing her violin.

Natalya loves creating her own products with the best natural and efficacious ingredients. She became one of the top leaders and directors as an independent brand partner in a natural skincare company. She became one of the faces of the company by working hard to earn the opportunity to be in a photo and video shoot that was offered for the select top leaders of the whole company. Her struggle with cystic acne and scarring led her to finally find a solution after 15 long years, thus leading to her mission to help others with skin concerns. She is empowering women to feel beautiful in their own skin and uses positive techniques to show that people are beautiful both on the inside and the outside. Motivating and uplifting others are the key components she builds all of her principles around, so that others can catch some light and begin to shine!

She hopes to share her story of heartache, failure, and hitting rock bottom, and how she scrambled out of it all, rose, took a stand and went after success with all her might, with others so that they too can have hope and follow her example of never giving up.

Natalya Melnik
205 Sackett Road
Westfield, MA 01085
413-896-3029
nskovorodina@yahoo.com
www.NatalyaMelnik.com

Aimee Carlson

From Franchise Owner to Network Marketing Professional

Who has heard, "Don't judge a book by its cover"? I know I heard this many times while growing up. But what does it really mean? Quite literally, it means we want to read and learn about the content of a book before we make a decision about it. And yet, I had been trying desperately to avoid this good advice my entire life! I wanted people to judge me by what they saw, not by how I felt on the inside.

By outward appearances, I had it all together. I had a very successful franchise business that my husband and I were in the process of turning over to our youngest son. I was teaching him the ins and outs of being an owner while I still had the reigns, so his transition would be smooth. My husband and I were traveling when we wanted and were spending our winters in a much warmer climate. In addition to the franchise business I owned, I had fallen into an accidental business and was growing a fairly large team. We had everything we needed and our financial future was secure. Out in public I was put together; hair always done, dressed nicely, makeup done. And all of this was in my 40's! My husband and I looked like we were living the dream life.

And yet, even with all of this, I felt stuck. I thought that if you really got to know me you would not like me. I was trying desperately to control everything and everyone around me so I didn't have to look at what was going on inside of me, and I also desperately needed others to approve of what I did.

I had reached a point with my team where we weren't growing; in fact, we were losing more team members monthly than we were adding. I knew that it was time to take a look at my leadership. I needed to figure out how to be a better leader, and a better person. I also didn't like how I felt on the inside. I was doing the same thing over and over and getting the same results. Sounds a little like insanity, doesn't it? I was truly at a point where I was either going to make a change or throw in the towel and quit.

This message hit me loud and clear after one of the annual events I did with my team. I was talking with my mentor about the things that went well and what we could do to improve for the next year. I was sharing with her that at this particular event I had felt very much at odds with my team. It had seemed that everything I wanted done, they thought should be done a different way. I will never forget her words to me. She said I needed to decide if I wanted to be right, or if I wanted my leaders to feel like their voices mattered. Ouch! Those words hurt. But they were the truth!

So began my journey. I started reading; not just reading, but putting what I was learning into action. I journaled a lot! The health and wellness network marketing company I am associated with today is absolutely incredible in offering opportunities to grow as a person. I made it a priority to attend an event every quarter. Twice I have gone to Oola Palooza, an event designed to help you create balance in the seven different areas of your life. I attended many seminars and weekend retreats. I invested in leadership training and workshops, especially from those who have already succeeded.

I have been blessed to learn from some of the best. Eric Worre is an industry leader, author, and accomplished trainer, and founder of Network Marketing Pro. I was able to attend one of his GoPro events that features the top performers in the industry. Eric has also been part of many of our company's international conventions, which I attend every year. My friend brought me to her mentor's house where Richard Bliss Brooke sat in the living room, sharing his best advice with about 20 of us. Mr. Brooke is a network marketing expert, best-selling author, and motivational speaker that people pay big dollars to learn from. After that weekend, I read and reread many of his trainings. I have also listened to CDs by Jim Rohn, one of the great motivational speakers and pioneer network marketing professionals.

Some of the first topics that I pursued focused on mindset. I read "Train Your Brain" by Dana Wilde, and I listened to "Conscious Language" by Marcella Vonn Harting and Robert T. Stevens; in fact, those CDs are still in my car and I listen to them frequently. Both of these speak to how we train our thoughts and words, and the power of our subconscious. I learned that the subconscious does not know the difference between what is real and what is not. For example, remember watching the movie "Titanic" with Leonardo DeCaprio and Kate Winslet? How many of you cried when Jack and Rose were floating on the wooden door in the freezing waters and Kate was telling him she'd never let go? I know I did, and like a baby! And then when she swam to get the whistle, I cheered her on! Watching these fictional events happening on the screen in front of us fills us with real emotions, because our subconscious does not know the difference.

There were many "tapes" playing in my head: those internal committees that are hard at work reminding us of what we can or cannot be, what we can or cannot do. These tapes develop throughout our lifetime, perhaps because of what someone said to us or what we decided for ourselves from our experiences. Those words or events may have occurred only one time in our past, but we hear the tapes thousands of times as we play the events in our heads; therefore our subconscious deems them to be real, and we feel the impact of the words over and over.

Growing up, my family was always involved with church. My grandfather was a minister, so the church felt like a second home. Wednesdays meant Trinity, which consisted of Bible school lessons and choir practice. Sunday mornings meant more classes and church service. My family was also very close, having lots of weekend gatherings. Holidays were always spent with family. When I was eight years old, my grandfather passed away from cancer. Just a year and a half later, my mother passed away from cancer also. And then, not even one year after her death, my grandmother passed away from multiple sclerosis. Suddenly, we didn't go to church anymore and we didn't gather with family like we did. In a period of less than three years my world was turned upside down. What once was, no longer existed.

There were two things I took away from this experience and carried into adulthood. First: don't love, because when you love someone they go away. Second: I must have done something very wrong for God to be so mad at me. As I continued through my high school years, I often heard: I could have done better. When I achieved something, whether it was scholastically or athletically, there was always criticism that it wasn't my best. So I developed a tape in my head that said, "You're not good enough." In growing up I decided that reality was far too hard and painful for me. I learned very quickly that drinking numbed the pain and took away how I felt, even if just for the moment. This caused me to make some pretty poor decisions and engage in questionable behavior, which led to shame and guilt. It was during this time of my life that I learned about secrets, and that we don't let people know everything.

From these books I learned that you can change your tapes, and that you speak what you want in your life as though it were. Richard Bliss Brooke tells us we can be our own producer and create a new movie. We have the ability to say we're not going to listen to negative self-talk. In conscious languaging we learn to remove words like try, want, and need, and replace them with "I can," "I choose," "I will," "I am," "I have." When we say words like try, want and need, we are coming from a place of lacking. We are telling our subconscious that we do not have, and that is exactly what it hears. Words like "I am," "I will," and "I choose" are words of creation and manifestation. What are we speaking over our lives, over our relationships, over our money, over our business? We get to choose!

I'm reminded of a time in my franchise business when were involved in a competition for our company's first ever National All Stars awards. Every store put together a five-person team to compete. The competition involved over 2,200 teams nationwide. It took a year to go through the brackets and get to the final three teams, who were then flown to our company's convention. We had one of the top three teams competing. The team members were treated like rock stars, with limousines and first-class hotel accommodations. They even had a press conference where each team was interviewed. Our convention was four days long, and the actual competition didn't occur until three days into the trip. So the entire three days, as I had been meeting new people, I was introducing myself as the franchisee of the winners of the first ever National All Stars, and introducing my team that way too! The competition was fierce and we knew we had given it everything we had. The team had no regrets and knew they were winners, no matter the outcome. So the next night at the awards gala, we waited while they announced all the winners for various awards. Finally, they came to the National All Stars. The third place was announced, so we were down to two teams left. When they announced the runners-up, we exploded: our team had won!! All the time while I had been introducing us as the winners, I had no idea that I was applying the principles of conscious language. However, when I learned about this principle, I could go back to this personal story as proof that it works.

I learned from listening to many Network Marketing professionals that in order for me to succeed in this business, I was going to have to look at who I was. And so I did. I spent months journaling and looking at what made me tick. I looked at my childhood experiences, what kept me awake at night, what stopped me in my tracks, and what held me back. I looked at the good things too: what values did I have, and what culture did I choose for our team to have? I looked beyond myself to the bigger picture.

I learned that every single time I feel "stuck" I am in my own head, not trusting in the process and in God. I spent time with a teacher who gave me a very simple exercise to do when I am in a place of having taken back control; this exercise has helped me over and over again. When I know I am in that place, I clench my fists as tight as I can and close my eyes. Slowly, I uncurl my hands and open them up with my palms facing upwards, and at the same time I say, "I give it all to you—my life, my work, my family—and trust that you will establish my thoughts, words and deeds." This is my version of practicing Proverbs 16:3.

I found that I learn through physically doing things. My husband and I learned in our marriage that when we became too emotional in a conversation neither one of us hears the other person. Since I was the one who typically did this the most, we came up with a solution we could do in the heat of the moment. We developed what we refer to as "Stop, Drop and Roll." During a conversation, if he saw me getting too emotional he would say to me, "Stop, Drop and Roll." And I physically would stop, drop down to the ground, and roll, just like we were taught in grade school. The simple act of doing this helped me reset my mind, we'd get a good laugh, and then we could carry on our discussion with both of us being heard.

I've learned a number of things from Eric Worre—truly one of the top inspirational speakers in network marketing. The first is: network marketing is absolutely the best business model in the world. It has created more millionaires than any other industry as a whole. It is not perfect, but it is better. I have been in the franchise model, and I can say from firsthand experience that if given the choice, I would choose network marketing every single time. The earnings potential is limited only by you. You can make this a full-time career, living a lifestyle that most don't dare to even dream of; or you can make this a part-time career, still living a better life than most have. The choice is completely yours. The industry has more personal development opportunity than any other industry! Being involved in network marketing is where I have grown the most and developed some of my strongest relationships. I also learned from Eric to know my numbers. I knew my franchise business numbers in my head; I could give you the rundown of what was going on in the business at any time. This business is no different: you need to know where you are in order to get to where you choose to be.

Another great storyteller I was introduced to early on in my network marketing career was Jim Rohn. There are a couple of stories that have really made an impression on me. He has a quote: "It is the set of the sails, not the direction of the wind, that determines which way we will go." This is so true, and when we can truly feel the meaning behind this we are set free. What I take from his story is that we all have the same opportunities; we all have trials and tribulations in our lives. The more you connect with people, the more you will find this to be true. I have found that I'm really not that unique; my story can be found many times over. We all have had things happen in our lives; the difference is in what you choose to do with both the opportunities and the trials. How are you going to set your sail? Are you going to allow yourself to become a victim, or will you choose to get up and move forward? In order to succeed in life, you need to continue getting up. Part of success is getting knocked down. If we aren't failing, then we haven't even tried.

You know we all have the same economy. I chose early on in my franchise life that I wasn't going to allow the economy to dictate if we were successful. I chose to focus instead on what we did control. I couldn't control what my competitors did or offered, but I could train my people to provide the best customer experience. By doing this, we stayed true to our values and remained financially strong while the ups and downs of the economy caused many competitors to struggle and even go out of business.

In my network marketing career, I have learned that everyone who is introduced to our company has the exact same opportunity I do. The compensation plan is the same for everyone, and the products are the same for everyone. It's what we choose to do with this opportunity that makes the difference: the setting of the sail.

This is where the story of the sower, as Jim Rohn tells it, comes in. In the Bible there is a story about a man sowing seeds. Some of his seeds were carried away by the birds. This means that some people who come upon our opportunity are not even going to want to hear it. Some seeds fell on rocky ground, so the plant started to grow but did not have deep soil to develop roots. Some people will join and use the products but never share. Some seeds grew on thorny ground, so the plants were strangled by thorns. We have those that come into our business with big dreams, but at the first signs of adversity they let those dreams fade. They are the ones that let every excuse win over choosing to change their life: I'm too busy, I have kids, I don't know anyone… and the list goes on. We all have the same hours in a day; it's what we choose to do with those hours that makes the difference in succeeding or not. There are women who work full-time, have 5-8 kids, homeschool them, AND build a network business. It can be done. And then the sower has seeds fall on fertile ground, and some of his seeds produced 30%, some produced 60%, and others produced 100%. Why is that? Jim says: it just is. These are the numbers. When we know this, we can stop trying to make the 30% become like the 100%; they never will, and that's ok. These numbers are the same across industries and hold true to our franchise business. We know that 30% of our customer base gives us over 80% of our business. If you work to change those numbers, you are spinning your wheels!

Last February I had the opportunity to attend one of our larger team's first-ever retreat, called Awaken. It was held in a beautiful log cabin surrounded by acres of trees and fields, with a huge fireplace that was going non-stop to keep us all warm. It was limited to 50 people, so it was a very intimate setting. Everything about the weekend was designed to make us comfortable; from the wraps that were given to us the first day, to the words of encouragement printed and strategically placed all around the cabin, to the home-cooked meals prepared and catered in. It was at this retreat that I truly had a couple of awakenings. That weekend I learned that as much as I tried, I was not in control, I never have been, and that I could let go. In letting go, I felt so much lighter; it was like I was pulled from a hole. My whole adolescent and adult life I had tried desperately to control every aspect, not just of my life but yours too! Now, this habit doesn't go away in one weekend; but knowing is the first step. There are days that I turn over everything quite easily, and then there are days that I am kicking and screaming! I am literally clenching my fists and releasing more times than I can count! I find certain circumstances much easier to turn over than others. For instance, business matters are much easier for me to turn over to God than personal issues. I find I need to stir that pot up quite well before I can turn it over to Him. The good news is I'm aware of it, and I know I have a choice today.

The bigger lesson I learned that weekend was the start of my story: Don't judge a book by its cover. We had just finished an intense emotional session, where the facilitator had asked for those willing to share how they felt. I was one of a dozen or so who shared. I told the others about the tapes that played in my head, the negative self-talk, how I had doubts about my abilities, and my fears of not being good enough. One of the other members at the retreat immediately shouted out, "How can you possibly feel that way? You run a successful company and have a large team. I've seen you speak and you are so confident! You are always beautiful!" Those words cut into me. I was so angry: How dare she question how I felt, when I was being vulnerable and sharing my fears! I wanted to say those words... but something kept me quiet. After that retreat, I kept coming back to her words.

Over the next several months following the retreat I had some very real personal life struggles. They weren't necessarily new, but they had come to a head. In really digging into this struggle, I realized that I wasn't letting go — I was trying to control. But more importantly, I was doing the same thing that gal had done to me: I was comparing my insides to others' outsides. When I allow myself to do this it is a recipe for disaster. I am not looking at what stresses might be going on in their lives, I'm not at a point where I can be empathic, and I am certainly not at a point where I can look for the good in that person. I believe, especially as women, we are always comparing ourselves to others. When we do this we are comparing our insides—how we feel—to others' outsides—how they look. When we judge a book by its cover we completely miss the authentic person, and we keep ourselves in a state of lacking. That gal at the retreat saw I looked put-together and confident; therefore I was. She had no idea how I felt inside. We are groomed for this: all you need to do to see it is look at what our forms of media deem desirable in our physical appearance as women.

I feel called to share my story with other women. I would like you to know that you have a choice. I was quiet at the retreat, but the words that gal said to me are why I share my story today. I would like you to know that all is not as it appears. We all have the same hours in the day and the same opportunities in front of us. Night will always follow day, just as Spring will always come after Winter. There are things that are certain; they just are. Accept those things. There are things we cannot change: other people. There are things we can change: ourselves. We have a prayer that we say, and I'll leave you with it. "God, grant me the serenity to accept the things I cannot change, the courage to change the things I can, and the wisdom to know the difference."

Aimee Carlson

From successful franchise owner to Professional Network Marketer, Aimee Carlson is able to share a unique perspective and demonstrate that outward appearances are not all they seem to be. Aimee heads the only 100% woman-owned franchise in her industry of over 2,200 service centers nationwide. She has been awarded Operator of the Year and several Customer Service awards, and has led her 5-person team to win the first ever National Championship as well as runner-up in the following year. Aimee's company has also been recognized with the Arlene Karlson "Heart and Soul" award for their contributions to their community, where their primary focus has been helping kids. They are proud to be partnered with Rock In Prevention, an anti-bullying and drug and alcohol prevention program, as well as MDA in raising funds to help send kids to summer camp.

As a Network Marketing Professional, Aimee has reached the top 1% in her industry. She leads a team of nearly 300, helping to transform lives! For the last four years she has created and produced an annual event for her team, and has also worked with other leaders in creating and promoting quarterly educational events. Aimee has attended numerous workshops and seminars for Network Marketing Professionals to further her skills and development. You can follow her story through her blog at www.aimeecarlson.com/blog.

Aimee Carlson is a wife, mother of three grown sons and grandmother to twelve. She lives in Iowa during the summer months and winters in Arizona. She loves to be outdoors, where you can find her hiking, kayaking, boating, biking, or reading while relaxing on the water. She and her husband love to travel and experience the beautiful outdoors, enjoying God's creation!

Aimee Carlson
10710 E. Gary Lane
Mesa, AZ 85207
515-240-1794
freedom@aimeecarlson.com
www.AimeeCarlson.com

Marcela Segal

A Woman's Journey of Courage and Purpose

How can someone who was born into a life of suffering and powerlessness become the narrator of their own life? How do we find internal peace when most of our lives have been ruled by outer chaos and the fear of the unknown? These are the questions that I posed to myself as a successful adult that was molded by their rambunctious upbringing.

I was born in the suburbs of Buenos Aires, Argentina, in 1967. I was the oldest of three daughters, but my parents might as well have been my siblings because they didn't treat me like a child. My mother was very progressive for that time and she dabbled in promiscuity and a feminine boldness that few women dared to explore. She spoke out against my father, who was a simple-minded man with a short temper.

As a child, I was thrust into a "flight or fight" lifestyle that has marked me until this day. My parents separated when I was twelve years old, at a time when it was not even legal to do so. I went through various incidents in which I was abandoned and left to fend for myself. At the age of fourteen, I started a relationship with a man ten years older than me. I was emotionally, mentally and physically abused for many years. My mother and father didn't even notice my pain because they were so removed from my life. I felt used and betrayed by my own flesh and blood. How could they care for me so little that they let a man ten years older than me control me and use me as he pleased?

I still get emotional at the anguish of having no voice to scream at that time in my life. Instead, I just closed myself off and put a mask on so I could stop getting hurt by the people around me. This led to a feeling of immense loneliness.

As I grew, I found myself becoming less submissive and less forgiving of the people who had done me wrong. I knew I had to build a future for myself. The problem was, I didn't know how to. Throughout my abusive relationship, I was supporting my mother—who always manipulated us with her illness—and sisters, while my stepfather was in jail. I figured I had to stay where I was because I felt responsible for my younger sisters and I wanted to protect them at all costs. I did not want them to go through the same things I had gone through in my life. Even though I was doing the right things, went to therapy and fought against the injustice, I did not know how to free myself from the only lifestyle I'd ever known.

My life reminded me of *The Odyssey* by Homer. I was exactly like Ulysses, fighting against each obstacle and monster with determination and bravery, hoping to find my way home. The only differences were that I knew the monsters personally and didn't really have a home to go back to—I just needed a safe place. Like Ulysses, I felt as though the whole world was against me, strong winds leading my ship astray and dangerous whirlpools taking people far away from me. As a teenager, I thought that living the way I'd been taught would lead to a path of happiness—building a family of my own, having a good career, and playing conventional roles.

I did various things to stay away from home as much as I could, but that left me at the mercy of my boyfriend, who would not allow me to have any friends. We took up bowling when I was fifteen. I fell in love with its beautiful simplicity. I could just play for hours without worrying about what happened outside in the streets of Buenos Aires. I had no idea how impactful bowling would end up being in my life, and I realize today how incredible life can turn out when we are given a chance and are alert enough to take it.

That chance appeared when I was twenty-three. After months of therapy and sheer courage I gathered the strength to break up with the man I had feared for so many years. Now I was able to confront my ex-boyfriend, and despite his complaints about me going alone, I went to Miami for the first time for a bowling tournament. I was completely mesmerized by the beauty of the city and the freedom that came with being there by myself. I distinctly remember the feeling of absolute happiness. I met people from my country that had big grins and free spirits, and I grew attached to them. I was enthralled by the ocean and the color of its waves as the sun glimmered on its surface. I was no longer Ulysses, a frightened sailor worn down by the ocean, trapped on board his own ship, begging to go home. I was Ulysses when he steps back into his kingdom after a decade, breathing the familiar fresh air—I had finally found my safe place.

One night in Miami, I had a dream that shook me to the core. I was floating over the city, a sense of lightness in my being that I had never felt before. I thought I was dead, but I wasn't afraid or confused; I was at peace. I had never felt this peace in my life, so I assumed that I had died. What a pure feeling that was, what a wonderful dream. In that moment, I realized what I had to do.

I found a way to get away from the chains of my past. This solved the main problems I had immediately, but it took me years to realize that I needed to learn about self-love and how to be happy with myself. First things first; I knew I had to move to Miami if I wanted a better life. I had read about moments like this in books: it is called "the call to action". It is the moment in a story where the main character is given an invitation to begin a journey that will resolve the conflict they are experiencing. That dream was my unconscious rattling my conscious self. It was time to be free.

Four months after I came back from that tournament I was ready to make my great escape into the unknown. I sold my car, my scooter, and the TV set in my apartment. I said goodbye to my family and I bought a one-way ticket to Miami and didn't plan to come back. Even though I had not been together with my ex for about a year by now, he kept threatening me and stalking me. We had a business in common, so I had a gripping sense of worry because I feared my plan wouldn't come to fruition. I feared he would hold me back and prevent me from leaving, and all my efforts would be for nothing. I decided to tell him that I was going to the dentist. He didn't suspect anything. I left him a short note saying, *We are finally free*. I never saw him again.

I didn't leave an address because I had no idea where I was going. I was Ulysses again, in my ship; but this time the ship was a plane and the ocean was the sky. I was not lost this time; I was drifting contently into an open horizon with endless possibilities. The feeling I had when that plane took off was almost indescribable. My chest opened to feeling again, my mind wandered watching the clouds floating, and I felt I was invincible. I had been reborn on that plane.

When I got to Miami, I found my way back to the Argentinians I had met four months ago. One of them called his mother and they gave me a place to stay out of pure generosity. I felt really lucky. I worked as much as I could in different jobs: as a waitress, a hostess, selling toys, then electronics, and the list goes on. I built my life with what I had, which was very little. I taught myself English by reading the dictionary, listening to songs on the radio, and doing crossword puzzles. I guess I was lonely, or I was already fulfilling the "good girl" path, so I got married to a good American man a month before Hurricane Andrew hit in 1992. When this scary storm came, he got drunk and left me alone with the dog in a pitch-black apartment. I knew he was not the man I wanted to spend my life with. About a year later I met the love of my life while I was visiting a group of friends. There he was, a man with long, curly hair and a poetic eloquence that stole my heart. I divorced the American and married the Argentinian man I was destined to be with. He was one of the best things that has ever happened to me.

My husband helped me get a job as a translator for the court, but it wasn't something I saw myself doing for a long time. He changed jobs and we moved to California so he could work in market research. We were struggling with money at that time, so I worked at a sandwich shop and I would bike all the way to work. We lived a thrifty life together and saved up for a better future every day.

When I got pregnant with twins, we decided to move back to Miami. A year later, my husband started his own market research company from the garage of our first owned house. I was having a crisis. I was thirty-six and had never had a chance to develop myself or think about what I wanted to do. But after going through the process of looking for our house, I went and got my real estate license so I could work from home. It gave me an opportunity to spend time with my children while also providing another income for my family. My husband's company started to grow very fast, so after doing a workshop on commercial real estate, I proposed to my husband that we buy a building so I could manage it and quit working for other clients. I built my company from the ground up and specialized in affordable housing.

I built my little "empire," as my daughter likes to call it, in just a few years. When my daughters turned seven, we moved to Argentina so they could experience our culture. I left the business with a management company, so I was again a stay-at-home mom. Going back home after so many years was very challenging for the whole family. Having more time and walking the streets of Buenos Aires again brought back old memories, but also a second chance to heal the past. I was diagnosed with Hashimoto's syndrome and soon after started having a persistent arrhythmia that did not seem to respond to any treatment. I didn't understand why I was experiencing so much discomfort now that I had everything I had ever wanted. I was very upset about this, so I decided to look for help. I looked for Beatriz, the amazing psychoanalyst that helped me get out of my predicament in my twenties — and I found her! After a few sessions with her I realized that I was living a lie, far removed from the revolutionary, passionate young woman I used to be.

Seven years later we moved back to Miami and I took over my business again. I still had the arrhythmia, but I was managing it a lot better.

I knew I had to try to be quiet and rest. I started doing yoga and took time to relax. I searched for things that interested me but nothing particular caught my attention. That is, until I started meditating and found some sense of peace; almost what I felt in that dream many years before. I wasn't in survival mode all of the time. The meditations led me to a workshop for women and it blew my mind. After that, I understood that what I had lost was simply connection. Being part of, belonging—that was what I needed. I stopped having my arrhythmias soon after.

I opened myself up to being vulnerable and started learning to love myself like never before. I learned about the power we hold back because of the fear we have felt in our pasts. I learned to use my voice to finally express myself after all those years of silence and being ignored. I watched as women rose up from the ashes of their tragic pasts and became the fire that illuminated the shadows. I felt as if I were a phoenix soaring over the blazing skyline. The world was mine; I just needed the connection with a community that understood me.

I began to notice a difference in the way problems and people around me changed; some people left, and new people showed up in my life. I engaged with the world differently because I related from a place of love and compassion. As I started to work on myself, my daughters began to take an interest in working on themselves too. They told me that they noticed a difference in the way I carried myself and how I acted as a mother. I experienced the ripple effect of love.

One day, I got an email from a wonderful organization called Global Sisterhood and I was invited to facilitate a circle. I started crying. That was my purpose—I wanted to facilitate and foster the experience of belonging and connection that exists amongst women and nature.

In March 2016 I started leading women's circles, and because that made me very curious, I started reading and researching and found Warrior Goddess Training by HeatherAsh Amara.

Last year I became a Warrior Goddess Training facilitator, and after walking on hot coals at the amazingly transformational retreats, I also became a Sundoor Firewalk instructor and an Artist of the Spirit Life coach. Walking on fire burned away many of my old beliefs, one by one, and showed me that this immense power was in me all of this time.

I became passionate about my life, and this has led me to meet many amazing women already leading the way. I have learned from them and healed so much, so now I feel the calling to pass it on to other women. In a few months I will open a space in Miami called "Light of the Goddess", where I plan to lead my women's circles and do workshops and events that foster personal development and spiritual growth.

I finally found my purpose in this world and I profoundly wish I could shed some light on other women's paths to find support and connection.

I strongly feel the feminine rising. Our role as women is crucial for society and the planet. We are the mothers that teach our sons to respect women and our daughters to respect themselves, and both to care for Mother Earth. By empowering ourselves as women we empower our children and those around us to do the same, no matter who they are. Simply put, I want to be part of the change that is already happening in the world.

Written by my daughter Sofia Segal.

Marcela Segal

With a traditional background in real estate investing, Marcela is the proprietor of an affordable housing business in Miami, Florida. After many years of successful work in this field, she eventually felt a longing within her heart that there was 'more', and so she embarked upon a personal spiritual journey more than a decade ago. She has since begun to lead monthly Women's Circles through the Global Sisterhood, and has become a Warrior Goddess Training facilitator, a Sundoor certified Firewalk Instructor, and is now fully trained in Spiritual Leadership, all under the powerful mentorship of HeatherAsh Amara.

Also, an Artist of the Spirit Life-Coach, Marcela is in the process of establishing a women's empowerment center, which is also located in Miami, Florida, called 'Light of the Goddess', where she will help women to find deeper connections with themselves and other like-minded women, to expand and support their spiritual practice as well as their overall education. This project is a dream come true where she fulfills her personal desire to create sacred space as she offers many classes, trainings, and ceremonies.

Future endeavors include organizing Light of The Goddess Retreats and completing her certification as a Yoga instructor and Health and Wellness educator with Claire Diab, founder of the American Yoga Academy and co-creator of the Chopra Center's Yoga program based on Dr. Deepak Chopra 'Seven Spiritual Laws of success'. Her future studies to become a teacher of Qoya with Rochelle Schieck and an Intentional Creativity teacher with Shiloh Sophia will allow her to offer these transformational practices at her Miami center in the near future.

Many women have contributed to Marcela's spiritual journey, and personal expansion, specially the heart-centered women of her monthly Circles that encourage her to keep going and to always follow her heart.

Marcela is passionate about her family, creating community, and also enjoys her organic garden, and spends much of her free time on a paddle-board in the Biscayne Bay.

Marcela Segal
8780 NE 2nd Ave
Miami, FL 33138
info@lightofthegoddess.com

Dr. Mimi Shekoski

Join Me for the Healthiest and Happiest Life Ever

How I Got into Holistic Health

Maybe because I talk straightforwardly, people often ask me how I got into holistic health and natural vision. I say, "It all started with bunions on my feet." You see, I gained almost 50 pounds when I was pregnant with my son. The weight from my big tummy was pressing down and gave me bunions on my feet. They were sticking out of my feet badly enough that my new husband kept saying they needed to be fixed with surgery. I always wanted to look fashionable, so I said to myself, "There's no way I'll wear those ugly surgery sandals at work for 6 weeks." So, I searched for a "natural way to correct bunions."

When I searched, *"The School of Natural Medicine"* showed up on my computer screen. The director, Farida Sharan, was shown on the front page. She had an amazingly warm smile and long silver hair, she wore a beautiful sarong, and her background was decorated with colorful silky fabrics. This was the summer of 2005 when I was working as a business development manager for Seagate Technology in Boulder, Colorado. Having a computer science and technology background, this image looked so foreign to me. Anyway, I was invited to her open house event. There I met Farida personally and other ladies of all ages, from early 20's to much older. Everyone who was there seemed to be searching for some sort of *self-healing*. Farida sat on a cushion in the front of the room and we sat comfortably anywhere in her living room. We each shared what was in our mind or what was going on in our life, and Farida shared her wisdom in her soft yet assertive voice.

I was so impressed by Farida and these holistically-minded ladies that I took time-off from my busy work schedule and attended a two-week-long summer school.

This summer school was the turning point of my life.

Farida told the summer school attendees that we were not allowed to consume alcohol, drugs, sugar, dairy, or meat during the school and for two weeks prior. I said to myself, "There's no way I could follow this rule for a month! I've got to have a glass of wine with dinner on weekends!" Well, I tried to follow the rules—except the alcohol part. It was also extremely difficult to avoid meat, sugar and dairy back then. I guess I was not the only one who didn't obey Farida's rule 100 percent. I remember a 21-year-old girl said to me during the summer school, "I went out with my boyfriend last night and smoked pot."

As for my diet back then, my idea of eating healthy was buying frozen vegetables, cooking them in the microwave oven, putting some sauce on it, and eating them. I was always health-conscious but had no idea what healthy eating entailed.

What I did and learned during summer school.

During the two weeks of summer school, we learned many holistic methods of self-healing. Farida rented a beautiful old barn with hardwood floors and let us decorate the whole place with colorful silky fabrics with sparkles, so it looked holistically colorful, inviting us to indulge ourselves in the hands of Farida's self-healing journey. We danced each day for the first three days, expressing different themes of the five basic elements: water, fire, earth, air, and space/ether. With music and our outfit colors matching the theme, we danced, relieved our feelings and pain, and hugged and held each other's hands. Although I was a happy person with a good new marriage, work, and life back then, my 13-year-old son mentioned that I looked different and happier when I came home each day after the summer school activities. Yes, I always liked to dance; but this was an eye-opening experience that I had not had before. I especially remember dancing with fire music, pounding our feet on the hardwood floor. On Air-Element day, we lay down on the colorful mat with essential oils applied to our feet, sparkles all over our hair, faces and clothes, and entered a transcendental meditational state.

We each made a Mandala. Interestingly enough, mine had two irises from both eyes combined into an eye shape with my family photos in the center. I had no idea that I'd be teaching natural vision!

I learned a few other *holistic healing methods* from Farida's summer school of natural medicine. We learned *herbal healing and raw vegan foods* from Brigitte Mars, nationally known herb expert and author of many holistic health and healing books, who had been living in Boulder. We had an excursion to another local herbalist's—Heidy's—house, where we soaked our feet in a barrel with herbs and warm water. It felt so good! We detoxed our kidneys with application of chopped ginger wrapped in a cloth around the lower back while soaking our feet in herbal water.

One day, Heidy guided us on a half-day hike on a Boulder mountain. Such fresh air; and the view was just gorgeous. Once we got to the top of the mountain, Heidy let us meditate for 30 minutes. I found it very difficult to stay still and calm. *This was totally opposite of what I do at work*, I thought. Every day, Heidy brought delicious raw vegan foods to the class; they were light, delicious, and easy to digest.

Farida gave us a lecture on *Iridology:* you can tell the health of your organs by looking at your iris with a magnifying lens. She went over everyone's, and mine showed a weak lymph system and digestive tract. I had to take some herbal powder to heal my body, but back then my body was so toxic that I couldn't even ingest these herbal products.

Another aspect of healing I learned, which changed my health and the health of others that I've worked with, was *Young Living therapeutic essential oils and their products.* Since then I've not touched any pharmaceutical or off-the-shelf drugs.

When I went back to work, many people commented to me that I looked radiant and well-rested.

Moving to the Midwest and making lemonade with lemons

In the spring of 2006, eight months after I attended the summer School of Natural Medicine, I had to relocate to a Chicago suburb due to my husband's new job. Many companies, including Motorola, were laying off employees around that time. Being a Stay-at Home Mom and Wife, for the first time in my life, was extremely difficult to get used to and I had to go through a self-identity crisis. Instead of losing myself in depression, I decided to make lemonade with lemons. I pursued my interest and passion I developed from Farida's summer school and started my holistic health program with the Global College of Natural Medicine and became a Holistic Health practitioner and Nutritional consultant. Rumor has it that the FDA closed holistic health schools, and this school was closed when I went back to get my PhD. I completed my PhD with the University of Natural Health.

Ever since 2005, since I attended the summer school of Natural Medicine, I've stayed so healthy that I've never got sick — not even a cold in the last 13 years. I sincerely owe my gratitude to Farida and other professors, including Dr. Andrew Weil, Dr. Deepak Chopra, Dr. Daniel Amen, and many other holistic health gurus whose teachings had a huge impact on the health and wellbeing of myself and my clients.

What about Natural Vision Improvement?

Although I was practicing natural health, like most people I didn't know we could improve our eyesight naturally without glasses, contact lenses, or surgery. Looking back, it must have been the Universe's calling on me to help people with their eyesight.

In the fall of 2012, I was scanning one of the holistic spiritual site's calendars and saw an event called "Improve Your Eyesight Naturally." I was using reading glasses and a magnifying glass to read prints smaller than 11-point font. I had to a use magnifying glass to read fine labels. As most of us have been told by typical eye doctors, I thought my age caused the deterioration in my vision, and nothing could be done except relying on glasses. I hated wearing glasses to read menus and labels, because they made me look and feel like a grandma—I wasn't one yet. Plus, with my flat nose, they kept slipping down to the tip of my nose. If I wore the metal-framed glasses to keep them up, then they hurt my ears and made bad dents on the sides of my nose. I didn't appreciate any of this.

Fortunately, my schedule opened up, so I attended the weekend workshop... and that was the end of my need for reading glasses. Being certified to be a natural vision teacher gave me more education and experience in healing people's vision issues.

I can proudly say that I've had incredible success in a short time frame, helping people to improve their distance and near vision so they can discard their glasses. It's been a wonderful and very rewarding experience. Many people who have worn glasses/contacts for most of their life can get rid of them within a few months.

Just like with everything else, I tell people that you have to have strong desire and intention for self-healing. You can restore your perfect vision at all distances by changing your vision habits and practicing simple techniques, so they become unconscious habit; that's all.

I feel so fortunate that I got into natural vision because I improved both my near and distance vision. Now I am 20/10 (much better than normal 20/20 vision) and can read font size 3 (even font size 2 in sunlight). Some people might say that's impossible, but believe me, it's not that hard to get your perfect vision back. Many people at all ages have done it, and you can too.

The natural vision improvement training is easy to learn, and anyone at any age—even after 70 or 80—can do it. And the best part is it's free, as you're using your own eyes to see. You will have good vision the rest of your life and *enjoy many other benefits* such as improved vision at all distances, reduced or gone astigmatism, better eye health, and better performance in sports and at work.

The other day, I asked a guy at FedEx to make copies of eye charts for my vision class. He asked me what these charts were. When I told him that they are used to improve eyesight naturally, he said, "Without surgery?"

Statistics have shown that about 90% of people in the US will wear glasses at one time or another. The American Academy of Ophthalmology (AAO) predicted that by the year 2050, nearsightedness (myopia) will be the leading cause of blindness.

It's not easy being in a profession which runs against mainstream vision care. The traditional health industry is becoming more aware of mind-body medicine and the benefits of healthy eating and exercise. However, natural vision, which was pioneered by Dr. William Bates about 100 years ago, is a very unfamiliar topic to almost all people, and it requires explanations of how we see, case stories, and testimonials. Another challenge is that people are used to quick fixes, and insurance supports mainstream treatments in vision care (and health). Most people don't want to be bothered with self-healing until they start having serious eye health issues. People contact me with bleeding retinas from eye drop injections; by then it's harder for natural healing to occur. As Benjamin Franklin said, "An ounce of prevention is worth a pound of cure." This is especially true when it comes to our vision and eye health.

Even with these challenges, I feel very blessed to have found my lifetime calling: helping people in the US and around the world to improve their vision and keep their eyes healthy.

The Best Ways to Stay Fit and Healthy

I strongly believe that healthy digestion is the key to staying healthy. Did you know 70 to 80 % of your immunity comes from your digestive tract? When we eat foods that are hard to digest, they not only cannot be assimilated well enough to give us the nutrients our trillions of body cells need, but they also stay in our intestines and make us fat and unhealthy, and even cause diseases in the body. Modifying your eating habits is not easy, but once you do it you will notice many ill symptoms go away. After 35 or 40, you also need to detoxify your digestive tract once in a while, unless you have always had a perfectly healthy diet all your life.

With my own experience and that of many others I worked with, I can attest that eating healthy and detoxifying your body periodically is the key to staying fit and healthy in this modern world. *Your eye health also comes from a healthy body.* The subject of good digestion, assimilation, and elimination is not a topic I want to talk about all the time, and yet it is the most important topic that all of us need to be educated on.

So, I wrote a book called "Lose Stubborn Weight: Become Fit and Super-healthy in 28 days (Sustainable and Healthiest Weight Loss, Lower Cancer Risk, Lower Blood Pressure and Cholesterol, Heal Diabetes)." You'll find the secrets to staying fit and healthy in this book. It's available on Amazon. Search with my name, "Mimi Shekoski", at Amazon.com and it'll show up at the top. It's a short, easy-to-read book and contains a ton of good information.

Power of the Mind for Good Vision and Health

You have probably heard the phrase, *"Your eyes see what your mind sees."* Most of us think we see with our eyes. Of course, the eyes are involved in seeing, but vision occurs mainly in the brain and mind! Our brain and mind are part of the nervous system, where the brain is the physical part and the mind is part of the invisible world consisting of memory, imagination, belief, feeling, attitude, and thoughts. The mind plays a more important role in vision than the brain. In fact, our mind is more powerful than the brain, because its intangible nature offers us an infinite amount of potential power.

Our eyes receive visual information in the form of light. The brain processes the information it has received through the optic nerves in the back of our eyes and makes image of it with the help of our memory, experiences, and imagination. That's why when babies are born, their eyes sense light from the start, but they have to learn to recognize different shapes, colors, Mommy and Daddy's faces, etc., using their memory and imagination.

William Shakespeare once said, "The eyes are the window to your soul." What this means is that your thoughts, attitude, and feelings can manifest on your eyesight. When it comes down to your vision, your physical, mental, and emotional state does affect your vision from day to day, from hour to hour, and from moment to moment. The research shows that our eyesight can fluctuate by as much as two diopters in a day. Thus, it's a good idea to avoid eye tests when your physical, mental, and emotional state is not optimal.

What Makes Eyesight Deteriorate?

There are three main causes of eyesight deterioration: prolonged visual strain, mental strain, and chronic emotional stress.

Visual strain is caused by staring; squinting; prolonged closeup work such as reading, studying, or working in front of a computer; and wearing glasses or contact lenses. Spending too much time doing closeup work results in losing accommodative power—your visual system losing its flexibility for seeing near to far. This is especially a problem for kids playing video games, causing development of myopia in kids.

Mental strain can come from trying too hard to see, feeling stuck, losing interest in life, having a rigid mindset, or overly long periods of mental exhaustion.

Kids usually start experiencing blurred vision between the ages of 8 and 12, because their nervous system is heightened during those years and they get sensitive about themselves and what's going on around them at home and at school. Kids also have problems at school, either when they get bored with a one-size-fits-all curriculum, or when learning unfamiliar things or subjects they are not good at disturbs their nervous system—thus, they cannot see the board ("it looks Greek to me"). Experiencing their parents' divorce, or physical/emotional abuse by a parent, teacher, or peers, can cause blurred vision as well. Many people I work with say, "Looking back, I know why my eyesight started getting blurry when I was a child. It's probably because I didn't want to see what was happening in my life."

Emotion plays a big role in vision. If you are going through emotional trauma, your vision will be blurry, and you may possibly even lose sight. One lady I saw lost her eyesight in one eye after the death of her son in a motorcycle accident. She stayed in bed for three months and got eye surgery, but nothing could bring her sight back. One of her friends suggested finding a holistic route. Just doing emotional freedom technique (EFT) for about 40 minutes brought her pain threshold down from 10 (out of 10) to 2. About two weeks later, we got an email from her and her husband saying that she got her sight back. That's how impactful our emotional stress is, and how powerful emotional clearing can be to our vision!

Negative emotions such as anger, resentment, hatred, fear, anxiety, grief, deep sorrow, or feeling abandoned can affect your vision, if you carry these emotions for a long time. Some of us experience some of these feelings. However, if these feeling do not go away and stay with you all the time, they get embedded in your subconscious mind and will affect your vision (and health as well). Thus, it's good to recognize the emotions you are feeling daily and reframe the thoughts and feelings.

Summary

In my past I led a very hectic, unhealthy, unhappy, selfish, and unbalanced life. I didn't know it back then; but now, looking back, I really did. Luckily, my life changed drastically for the better. My current life makes me feel like I am among the healthiest, happiest, and most victorious people. This, of course, didn't come to me easily. Many times, I have felt like I joined a clan most people don't accept as the norm. Through all that, I am so glad that I took this path and that I am able to help people find better life and vision.

Dr. Mimi Shekoski

Mimi Shekoski, Ph.D., is a Natural Vision Improvement teacher/coach, Natural Health doctor, author, Holistic Health & Wellness expert, a Neuro Linguistic Programming (NLP) practitioner, and an Emotional Freedom Technique (EFT) practitioner.

Dr. Mimi specializes in renowned Bates Method of Natural Vision Improvement and Natural Healing of the Body, Mind, and Emotion. She offers individual coaching, workshops, seminars, and online video programs on myopia (nearsightedness), presbyopia (poor reading vision after 40), astigmatism, computer eye strain, and more.

Have you met people who are so passionate and enthusiastic about what they do that they inspire you to take an action? That's Dr. Mimi! She is very passionate about educating and helping people make meaningful changes to achieve a healthfully balanced life. Since 2006, she has influenced many people's lives, improving their eyesight, health, and wellness, by using her holistic method and mind-body-emotion healing modalities.

In her previous life, with her master's degree in computer science, she worked in various high-tech companies including NASA. From her many years of people-interfacing and managing experiences, she has a keen sense of how to inspire people to achieve their optimal vision and health goals naturally and successfully.

People describe Dr. Mimi as a super-talented, caring, energetic, and inspiring person with insightful knowledge and experiences on natural vision, health, and wellness.

She lives in a Chicago suburb with her awesome husband and a grown son.

Dr. Mimi Shekoski, PhD, MS
HBN INC
4314 Carlisle Drive
Crystal Lake, IL 60012
815-219-7897
DrMimi@HappyEyesight.com
www.HappyEyesight.com
www.NaturalVisionOnline.com

Bron Watson

Success Despite Adversity:
The Miracle of The One Percent

You never know how strong you are until you have no choice.
—Bron Watson

There will never be a time when life is simple. It's complicated and messy, and things don't always work out the way we want. Bad things happen to good people and it sucks. Whether you are an entrepreneur or an entrepreneur-at-heart, it is at these times when things get chaotic... If this has happened to you, I am sure you can feel that challenge in your gut right now. If not, it's time to prepare. The old saying "forewarned is forearmed" absolutely nails it.

In your own business, when you have to play the roles of CEO, financial controller, admin and coffee runner, all at the same time, adversity can bring everything crashing to the ground... especially when there is no Plan B. In addition to business acumen, entrepreneurship requires the courage to back yourself when others cannot see your vision. It's more than self-help, more than economic outcomes and business growth strategies. Entrepreneurship is more than business—it is a way of life.

Year after year, the number of people running their own businesses continues to grow. Recent research by the Global Entrepreneurship Monitor (GEM) shows that just under one fifth of working age adults across 54 countries are engaged in entrepreneurial activity, with North America having the highest early stage entrepreneurial activity rate.[1] Exciting new insights show that many of these new businesses are being triggered by opportunity, rather than the more traditional impetus of necessity.

It is in times of hardship and adversity, when there is no Plan B, that the intersection of business and life becomes blurred and difficult to manage. It is knowing what to do when adversity strikes, when you're caught in the business, that is important. But because of the overlap, it's not always clear if it is entrepreneurial savvy or self-help skills that will make the difference. In Australia, more than 60% of small businesses fail in the first three years because of the high level of adversity and challenges. While there are no statistics on the way these challenges evolve on a personal and business level, many entrepreneurs the world over experience adversity, hardship, cash-flow challenges, time limitations, illness, and stress and exhaustion caused by trying to run a business while leading a fulfilled life. I never for one second would have believed I could be a statistic, or that adversity would strike... but it did.

Like many who have hit their fifth decade, and after the birth of my fifth son, I decided it was time to try my hand at running my own business. I had a few friends who had their own businesses, and it looked pretty easy to me. It couldn't be that hard, right? How naive was I at the time?

With zero experience and only a few dollars in my bank account, my first business, Nurse Power, was born. I am a Registered Nurse and Clinical Educator, and with a laptop and the internet, I built a thriving community online for nurses across the globe with around 25,000 followers. The personal challenges faced by nurses do not discriminate by culture or country.

Once Nurse Power was up and away, I was often asked: How does a nurse not only start a brand new business, but build it to become wildly successful? It was from here the "Bron Watson" consulting brand was created. In my career as an educator and entrepreneur I have worked with thousands of people to help them overcome life's challenges and to help their businesses to

1   Global Report 2017/18 The Global Entrepreneurship Research Association. www.gemconsortium.org/report

thrive. I have had the privilege of combining education and entrepreneurship, and providing education, support and inspiration to thousands of entrepreneurs through personal mentoring and on-line programs. During these times, the one thing I noticed all of these entrepreneurs struggling with is how to work successfully when adversity strikes... when there is no Plan B... when there are many solutions available but few results.

In 2016, the first of a series of adverse situations began for me. I ordinarily live in Australia; however, we took our family to London for just under six months, as a family health issue had become quite serious. As a parent, there are times when you have to take drastic action to do what is needed. This was one of those times. There's nothing like living in a foreign country—even though we all spoke English—having clients on the other side of the world, and dealing with time zone differences. I would stare across to Greenwich at the Cutty Sark, one of many famous landmarks in London (we had rented an apartment in Island Gardens), wishing I was home in Australia while looking at one of the most famous rivers in the world, the Thames. Travelling the world was on my bucket list, and something I had longed to do. Now that I was there, and it was not working out the way I thought it would, all I wanted to do, was to get home to my safe and simple life.

It was during those dark times that I began to take a closer look at what entrepreneurship means...believing in yourself to create something from nothing. Although there is a plethora of books available to the entrepreneur, the focus is usually on either professional or personal development, rather than this messy, blurred intersection in which many people find themselves. It's when you're caught in your business, when things go wrong and not to plan, when the help you need is not so easy to find.

My breaking point came in September 2017, with a diagnosis of breast cancer. Overnight, my world went from running two businesses, raising five children, healthy, active, madly working and doing what needed to be done to support our family, to being told that I needed significant surgery followed by months and months of chemotherapy and radiotherapy. It's what I call a left turn: you think you're going in one direction and you want to turn right, but suddenly the GPS takes you into a left turn and you don't know where you're going.

Being thrown into the health system while coming from nursing myself was a shock. After educating students and patients alike for more than two decades, I realized the enormity of the words I had shared so easily. Normal became a thing of the past. Life went from working towards a goal, following a clear path I had set myself, thinking I knew what was coming next... to a place where nothing was normal, nothing happened the way I thought it would, and my brain scrambled for anything resembling "normal". Adversity does that. It takes away the certainty, and you're left with an extremely vulnerable situation.

During those months of treatment, every single time I would realign, reassess, and re-plan, something would happen — whether it was significant reactions to chemotherapy and sickness, or having to move twice in five months (both times during chemotherapy). I'd be on that damn left turn yet again, with my trajectory and my world turned upside-down. Bad things happen to good people, and you don't know how strong you are until you have no choice.

The biggest challenge here, of course, was that I only had myself and my inner thoughts to pull me through. The dark times staring over the River Thames were not so bad after all, and neither was having three children under three; that had been a walk in the park compared to this. Like so many women, the challenge was this: my focus had been on looking after my family, my friends, my clients, and my community, with all my heart and soul... and little time spent looking after me. It took a mammoth adverse experience with disease for me to realize I had been living life all wrong.

There is nothing like post-chemotherapy illness to bring you back to the present, where you only have the moment, where there is no choice but to sit and survive. You only have what is going on right now, and it is simply impossible to look towards the future. It was during the times of not being able to walk around, having no hair, and being bright red due to the reactions to the drugs that I realized my focus on life had to come back to me. I had to come back to myself first.

This lesson has been one of the most incredible I could have ever experienced. When all your energy is given to other people it can be really dangerous, because it leaves you with nothing left in the tank when things go wrong. During this time, I allowed myself to reflect, to slow down to what I call "living in second gear," and to really notice what was going on. My life had been lived in top gear, where the speed meant I achieved a lot in my career, my business, and my bank balance. But as with anything, there is always an equal and opposite reaction... It meant I lived looking into tomorrow, next week, next year, rather than enjoying and being grateful for the moment I have today.

I spent time on myself, because I had no choice. I couldn't spend it on anyone else. I journaled. I realized that running a business in top gear, always planning, always looking ahead to something in the future, isn't the way to do life. Life is about being in the present, because tomorrow is guaranteed to no one.

At that time, I began to focus on the good cells, not on the bad cells, in my body. Not on the cancer cells, but on the 99.9% good parts of my health and my body, my brain. As they say, what you focus on is what you get. But it's more than that. It's about looking at how you act and react to a situation or an experience. You can either come to each experience from a place of love — which is powerful — or from a place of fear — which is powerless. Rather than spend my time projecting and resenting and wishing it wasn't happening to me (although of course there were times when I did) I began to focus on what I could do for now. I focused on who I needed to be in the present to be able to work through the adversity, because it wasn't going away.

It is at these times that you can either blame someone or something for what has happened, or you can take responsibility for how you act or react to the situation. It's not being responsible, but it's taking responsibility in the here and now, and into the future... responsibility of behavior.

The Miracle Of 1%

Reading most self-help books, the big recommendation is to set a goal... a big one, without a glass ceiling. That is true; I definitely believe in having a purpose and mission in life. The thing is, it can be completely overwhelming when it comes to actually doing the work during times of adversity. Focus on what needs to be done, one percent at a time. Rather than looking to the future and focusing on your big goals—even though they are fantastic and of course you really should have them—bring it back to the present.

Bring it back to the miracle of one percent... because when adversity strikes, it may be all you have. It's while focusing on the one thing, the one percent of working towards your goal, that small incremental change happens, one percent at a time. It could be taking a 10-minute walk when you weren't walking at all. It could be attending a reiki session or massage and relaxing and being in the moment for just one hour a week, when you were never doing that for yourself before.

You may ask... Why? Why focus on one percent, when so often we are asked to do three main tasks, or to make a significant change in how we do life? The reason is simple: a focus on one percent is doable, achievable, one day at a time. It allows you to live in the present. And the best part is, all those one percent's add up. They end up adding up to massive change, and achievement... success despite adversity.

Slow Down to Speed Up

As I mentioned before, it's consciously living in second gear. Second gear will give you results far greater than being in top gear, where life can be too busy, with too much going on... especially when focus stays on other people, experiences, and the future. Second gear means you can stop and, as the saying goes, "smell the roses." You can slow down and appreciate every single moment. Just like the good cells, focus on what is important, and let go of what is not.

Easy to say... hard to do.

The part where many people give up, way too soon, is what I call the gap between the *"thought"* of what you want and actually *"doing"* it. For many people, there are millions of thoughts of wanting to do something or to "be" something, and the action either does or does not follow. Success means bringing it back to what is real and what will work for you right now, so that you can then go and achieve the things that you really want.

When I was diagnosed with breast cancer, a lot of my energy was consumed by my fear of dying. I often projected a future without me in it, with my boys being left without a mother (my youngest was only eight at the time). When adversity strikes, and it strikes hard, it can upend a life in an instant.

The serenity prayer is believed to have been written decades ago by Reinhold Niebuhr, a prominent Protestant theologian of the 20th century (although there has been recent speculation about other potential authors). In 1942, Alcoholics Anonymous (AA) began using the prayer in a version that reads: "God (or however you see this entity), grant me the serenity to accept the things I cannot change, the courage to change the things I can, and the wisdom to know the difference."[2]

This is an ongoing process and something I believe helps us focus on just today. It takes daily work towards making it a habit, just like cleaning your teeth. It's about being in control when life is in chaos. It's now more important than ever that focus remain on the here and now, on the present filled with compassion and being grateful for the day.

Like anything, this type of transformation was, and continues to be, a work in progress. I still go through times of sadness and loss... but what used to be days of fear are now only moments in time. I now see my behavior for what it is, and I have a much greater awareness of what I can control and what I cannot. Yes, of course there are times when I am terrified that I may die early. The thing is, we all will die. It's a matter of living for the now, while working towards the future... it's about today being the best day ever. Tomorrow will

---

2   Alcoholics Anonymous. 2001. Big Book 4th Edition. Alcoholics Anonymous World Services, Inc. USA

look after itself.

Just Let It Be

The biggest lesson has been taking the time to really focus on the good cells and starting to look after myself, in business and in life, before anything and anyone else. It's that letting go. Before this time, I had tried and failed many times at working through letting go.

A few years ago, I attended a sales training event. It was a retreat-style gathering where a number of very successful entrepreneurs came together to work on their businesses, make sales, and focus on getting the job done. Pressure was high during the event. There were business owners that were making over $2M per annum. Talk about feeling out of my depth! The fear of looking like a fraud, of not being good enough and not fitting in, ran constantly through my mind. There were some serious players in the room, and then... little old me. Well... at least that is what it felt like at the time. During the week, one of the leaders opened up his laptop and started playing "Let It Go" by Idina Menzel, from the movie *Frozen*. Now, as a mother of five, I had heard this song many times. Before I knew it, I was humming along and wishing I could be teleported to the Disney Kingdom of Arendelle to hang out with Elsa and Anna. As the tune played in the background and the eyes of my fellow attendees glanced towards me and then away, I realized one thing: I had no idea, not one single thought, of how to "let it go." It was as if I was in another paradigm, and I was watching my life on TV.

The question is this: How do you "let it go" when you have zero understanding of how to make this concept a reality? Or, more importantly, to make it a livable part of everyday life? What I believe to be true... for me at least... is this: rather than "let it go," "just let it be." By creating habits based on the serenity prayer, I have been able to "let things be."

Being an entrepreneur means being fairly used to having things not work out the way you want them to. If you've started a business, you'll understand this. Creating something from the bottom up is nothing short of a phenomenon.

Results begin and end with you... but because of this, at any time something can change and send you and the business off on another tangent.

This, in turn, means heightened emotions. Some come from a place of love, yet others from a place of fear... feelings of resentment, projection, shame, blame, obsession, and self-pity, to name a few. Like any emotion, they're all a part of this thing called "life." The challenge is, of course, that these feelings can lead to letting go of the wrong thing, which is... responsibility.

Take Note

As the chief coffee drinker of my business—this is my title—it is up to me how I deal with fear-based emotions. I have two choices... do I control them, or let them control me? The way to start controlling fear-based emotions is to simply take note. Slow down and ask: Why do you feel this way? Is it your responsibility to own these feelings?

I liken it to being on a roller coaster. You get on, and round and round you go, upside down, spinning all over the place. There are times when you just want to get off. Get off for a while. By all means, have a pity-party... I sure have had loads in business and life. Take note of what is going on, and how you feel. But above all... get back on. It's your life, your business, your career... and only YOU can make the changes needed to live in a place of love rather than fear. Focus on looking after the cells you can control... For me that now includes good nutrition, mindset, wellness, exercise, and self-care. When the focus is filled with these, life is lived with feelings like compassion, gratitude, flexibility, honesty and community.

Steps to Get Started

1. Buy yourself a new journal. Make sure it is in your favorite color. It's time to start writing down thoughts and feelings every single day. Details on what and when to write is listed below.

2. On any given day, emotions and feelings will skyrocket, all spinning around in your head... whether it be in response to being stuck in

traffic or to major adversity. This is the time to slow down, pause, and focus on the gap between your thoughts and your actions. Take note. Whenever there is a moment, or an experience or flush of emotion, make a note on your smartphone or notebook. Use the following questions to guide your journaling.

Ask yourself the following four questions:

- What is going on?

- What am I feeling? Why?

- Is there anyone who can assist me?

- How do I want to feel?

3. At the end of each day, journal these experiences. Take note of your feelings, and describe them as best you can... the more specific the better. This is not the time for a solution. This is a time to simply take notice, write and acknowledge the truth for what it is. There is no right or wrong... it is time to simply let things be.

Creating awareness of your feelings and emotions—which are attached with daily life events and experiences—gives you the ability to focus on what needs to be done, so that you get the results you are looking for. You could be pursuing a health goal, a business goal, a travel or fitness goal. The result is not as important as the process to take you there.

4. Read what you write. Create a new story to go with the situation. Write that down and read it aloud. Share it with an accountability partner.

5. Write down this new story as a goal, as if it were now. Again, be as specific as you can be.

6. Break the goal into segments: up to three or four at most.

7. Break these segments into action steps, planning out what you will do. This is what fills the gap between thought and action... all based

on how you want to feel. Tackle them one percent at a time.

8. Rinse and repeat... Every. Single. Day.

9. Any change can be painful. It takes commitment, energy and time to create a one percent miracle. Do not give up.

Honesty is key here. Committing to the process of finding your success despite adversity takes time; it won't happen overnight. There is no silver bullet that will take out the fear monkey in life, but by focusing on the good cells, and removing the focus from the negative or bad, fear will no longer have the power you thought it did. The negative will become powerless.

If you would like further resources and help in implementing these steps into. Your everyday life, or if you are looking for an accountability partner, head on over to www.bronwatson.com/successresources. Here you will find further free resources to assist with this process, and the opportunity to join our private Facebook group for accountability and support. I hope to see you there. I will be in the group regularly and I am happy to connect.

With one percent incremental changes that compound over time, as you learn these new strategies to achieve success despite adversity in business and in life, you too can become a member of the miracle one percent club.

Bron Watson

You don't know how strong you are until you have no choice. It's not until things go terribly wrong, and you do what needs to be done, that you realize it is possible to have success despite adversity. That there is no plan B, and all you've got… is you.

Like many, Bron Watson had a burning desire to strike out on her own. After the birth of her fifth son, Bron braved the entrepreneurial world and started her first business. Entrepreneurship is more than business; it is a way of life. It is believing in yourself to create something from nothing. That way of life came to a grinding halt with a diagnosis of breast cancer. The subsequent treatment of surgery, chemotherapy and radiotherapy meant that running a business and simply living life became all but impossible.

This story provides the reader with step-by-step directions on how to overcome adversity, keep focus on the "good cells," and find the strength to work through a challenge using the miracle of the one percent.

Bron Watson began her career in nursing in 1989, developed her passion for education and completed a Master of Professional Education and Training in 2017. During these years, Bron has maintained a dual career in marketing and nursing, resulting in a unique combination of education and entrepreneurship.

During the past seven years, Bron has provided education, support and inspiration to thousands of entrepreneurs through personal mentoring and online programs, so that they, too, can be successful and achieve their dreams. As Bron will attest, it means a change in the way life is lived, with a focus on the now. It takes living life in second gear, where results can be achieved without stress, confusion or being overwhelmed.

Read how one Aussie mum has found success despite adversity, and how you can too… one percent at a time.

Bron Watson
PO Box 5563
Port Macquarie NSW 2444
+61 433 201 510
bron@bronwatson.com
www.BronWatson.com

Sharon Whitehead

My Lonely Heart Restored

Being the oldest of five kids in a religious Christian home was tough. It was church twice on Sundays — we attended several different churches, schools and varied Christian meetings. They ranged from Calvinistic to charismatic, from extremely legalistic to a cultish group. In the confusion, I didn't know what I believed. However, I did know that I was guilty until proven innocent. I knew that others were more important than myself, and if I had something to say, it was generally wrong. If I threw up, I better get a rag and get it cleaned up; we were healthy and not allowed to be sick.

Dad worked hard in his landscaping business while rebuilding our run-down farmhouse, away from any neighbors. Mom was home trying to keep everything organized. Because we lived so far from school, we were the first on the bus and the last off. I don't remember eating breakfast. We had a small lunch and when we returned home from school, we were allowed to eat some crackers or an apple. When Dad finally got home, Mom would give him a peck and return to making dinner. Finally, we could pray and eat our basic meal together. If our eyes were opened at any time during the prayer, my mother knew because she was peeking at us. As soon as the prayer was over, we were sternly told that she knew our eyes were open and we needed to keep them closed.

I longed for my Dad's approval and would do anything to keep him happy. He had humor and twinkly eyes that I enjoyed when he was around his friends. However, when he was home, he was usually tired and just wanted to read and rest.

One cold and wintery morning, somehow, we were late and missed the Christian school bus. My mother was yelling as she packed the baby and we all got into the station wagon. On the long ride we were told several times how this was our fault and it could never happen again, or we would be in big trouble. Being the caretaker in the family, I thought long and hard about how to make sure we would never miss the bus again. That evening, I found the yellow legal pad and wrote the bus driver a note. "Mr. Bus Driver, just so you know, we NEVER miss school. We are ALWAYS there, so don't EVER leave without us being on the bus again, or something bad will happen."

In the morning, I tucked the tightly-folded note in my coat pocket. After the bus driver gave a cheery "good morning", I handed him the note and said, "Here's something for you to read." Later that evening, my dad yelled as my mother stood watching. I studied the wallpaper design to tolerate being belittled and wrong again. With them glaring, he handed me the paper and said that I would have to eat my words. I stood there chewing my note of protection with them watching, until I swallowed it. I didn't cry, but I knew that I would never treat my children like this, ever!

My mother was a bundle of nerves and barely seemed to be enduring life. It seemed that my father was oblivious to anything that was going on in the house. It was as if they had an emotional divorce. My mother liked order, and with the part-time remodeling project, things were never in order. I don't know how she did it. We switched rooms a lot and had a make-do kitchen. Physically and emotionally, I wasn't sure where I could go and who I was. We lived a chaotic life. In her frustration, Mom would yell, chase and beat us with a three-sided ruler. She called it chastising. She said that's what it was called in the Bible. I was called Goofus and Missy to keep me in my place. She yelled that she was going to knock my head off and it was going to be rolling down the hill. I was sure that she was sorry she ever gave birth to me. I believed that I was a disappointment to God. But the pictures and stories that I heard in Sunday School of Jesus gave me hope.

While attending a public school, I learned that being beat was unacceptable and that we could call 911. Being the family protector at 13 years old, I yelled at my mom to stop beating my younger sister. I began taking pictures of the abuse on my little Kodak camera and was going to call the emergency number. Mom immediately stopped and came running after me, hung up the phone, grabbed the camera and took the film out.

While attending church, my mother would cry. She was trying to figure out her own relationship with God. Mom had a hernia operation followed by a nervous breakdown. She was exhausted after trying to keep order in our lives. As she recuperated on the couch, she read Christian books and cried some more. Being the oldest, there was now plenty more for me to do in the house. I resented being an 8th grader caring for the house chores and my mother. I pulled hairs out of my body with a tweezers to relieve the stress. Trying to survive and figure out my family, I ordered the magazine "Psychology today" and bought my own food with babysitting money.

I was jumping off of a hay cart into the tall weeds when my foot came down on a large rusty piece from the trailer. I was in extreme pain but unable to cry. Gnats swarmed around the blood. Eventually, my father slowly walked out. He was not happy about having to go to the ER, and we sat in silence the entire way. Again, I was a burden. Later, I was informed by my mother that I was being punished by God because I had a bad attitude and needed to understand how she felt. I have since learned that rules without relationship equals rebellion.

Trusting only in myself, I moved out at 17, At 18, I met a janitor while working in a nursing home. He was gentle, with a twinkle in his eye, and the older people laughed at his jokes. At the time I couldn't equate it to what I wanted in my father, but it was. He was 43, divorced, and already had five kids, one older than me. He was a charming manipulator who wanted to marry me and have a baby. Of course, I was not going to marry him... until I was 19. He told me I wouldn't get pregnant, but he knew I was pregnant before I did and already had names picked out.

I didn't want to get married, and I didn't trust anyone else to raise my baby. My children were going to know that they were loved, special and cherished. I would spend time playing, reading and singing with them. We lived below poverty level. While my husband took several entry-level labor jobs, they didn't seem to last. I took in kids, did ironing and cleaned homes to stay afloat. We were involved in church so my kids would have a solid foundation.

I was trapped, so if I had more babies, what difference did it make? I thought that I loved him, and did my best to prove that we would make it. I would not be a failure and then another statistic. Yet, I was worried that I might catch a disease from my husband when we slept together.

It was Christmas Eve several years later, and the small Christmas tree was lit. The family—my husband and four kids—decided to open our few gifts. I was shocked that my husband got me a gift. It was a size 10 jean dress. What? I was a size 20-22. I was told that if I would lose weight that I could wear it. I had been existing and was numb to the world; I wondered why I was even alive. Yet, I felt my spirits drop even further after hearing myself being mocked again.

Later, when the rest of the family was downstairs watching a movie, I numbly walked into the bathroom. I was going to be gone; nothing else mattered anymore. I had gone through the kids' memory box one last time. It wasn't that I wanted to die; I just couldn't take the emotional pain anymore. It was unbearable, being told that I was going crazy. There were some good times, but it hardly balanced the emotional abuse that I knew.

I looked into the mirror one last time and then yelled out, "Jesus, please pray for me!" I had never said those words in my life! I curled up on the couch and sobbed while watching a tape of the "Young Messiah," and felt God's loving and strong arms hold me in a way that I had never been loved or understood before.

I had my husband move out and was released from the mental health hospital that I put myself in. A friend said, "Let God take you back to a time in your life where he wants you to go". Shaking with fear, my mind returned to our childhood backyard with the hanging tire swing. I was in the fifth grade, giving Jesus a ride as I sang him a song. I figured that he would like to be cared for: if he was like me, he needed to be cared for too. As I told this to my friend, I was so proud of myself. She then asked me to let Jesus get off, and for me get on the swing and allow Jesus to push me. I cried, saying that I didn't know how to allow others to care for me, and certainly not Jesus. Finally, I was able to picture myself doing it. I didn't know that Jesus would now be my best friend and care for me in an incredible way.

I checked out a Catholic book about Jesus' mother Mary and all that she had to live through. I learned how Jesus cared for my soul. I was hooked, not on religion, but on a relationship. He was my best friend. I felt loved, surrounded and understood in the most incredible way. "Cast all of your anxiety on him because he cares for you." I Peter 5:7 NIV

Since the church didn't seem to understand what I was going through, Jesus, therapists and doctors became my best supporters, helping me figure out who I was and how this had happened to me. I knew that I would be ok.

Today, I am a speaker, author, certified trauma recovery coach and a registered nurse. I have a wonderful husband that adores me, and we enjoy many grandchildren. My purpose is to share a relationship with Jesus vs. being religious. I'm reminded of my swing experience, and thank God for Jesus and his love for me. I made it through the tough years of single parenting by the grace of God.

I learned that we repeat what we know. I've studied my parents' histories and know that they did the best that they could considering their own backgrounds and upbringing. Just as I did the best that I could with my kids, they too have memories of being hurt. I love my parents very much, and miss my father who has passed on to heaven. Life is short. We only have this moment to learn who we are and grow into who we were made to be. A victorious and overcoming woman who lives in a loving relationship with God.

Sharon Whitehead

By the age of 50, having suffered a stroke and a diagnosis of fibromyalgia, Sharon's days of working as a registered nurse, or any constant job, were over. Feeling lost, bitter and angry, she wondered what was next. She cried, begging God to tell her the purpose for still being alive. Hadn't going through abuse, neglect and trauma in her life been enough? Why was everything her fault? When would she feel loved?

To encourage herself and others dealing with emotional and physical pain, Sharon began a Facebook page called "Purpose Beyond the Pain." A safe place to share, be accepted, and learn while applying self-compassion. She also led "The Journey", a group of overcomers dealing with heartaches, learning to trust God and others. She believed that there was strength in a positive, caring and honest community.

Today, Sharon is a masterful speaker, author, coach and RN. She understands that the body, spirit and mind are intricately connected into one being. She is also a certified trauma recovery coach. She believes that when a person experiences trauma, the body absorbs and reacts while causing physical issues. She loves to laugh and dance, and has been called a" ray of sunshine" on a dark day. Her ability to find the positive, to help others with personal development, and to match the efforts of individuals wanting help are a few of her strong points.

Share the hope! Are you ready to be inspired, challenged and empowered to take control of your life? Sharon will speak honestly and with empathy. She will connect and liberate your audience. She believes that you too can be free from being beat down and totally misunderstood. You are invited to call and hear her story as she offers hope, healing and vision to your group.

Sharon Whitehead
Purpose Beyond the Pain
6890 Camino Del Rey Drive NE
Rockford, MI 49341
815-708-3068
sharonsue40@gmail.com
www.SharonWhitehead.com

Briane Amodeo

The Not Relationship and

How to Get Through It

Sitting next to my dying grandfather, I took a call from a woman I had never met who lived in Florida. The only other thing I knew about her was we had one mutual friend: the man I had been with for the past two years who had suddenly told me through a text that we would never be more than friends. One day I'm telling him I need him for emotional support, and the next I'm fuming that I just got off the phone with his fiancée.

My heart sank. How could I be with someone for two years and yet know so little about him? The number of things we turn a blind eye to, all because we think it's love. All the wasted emotions and efforts on someone who would never appreciate what was right in front of him. It breaks my heart to think about the time spent away from my Nonno to deal with that situation, and it being the last few days I would see him alive made it that much worse.

I knew better. The red flags were coming from every which way. Everything was always on his terms. When things got emotional, he disappeared, only to reappear and apologize. He would constantly be on his phone, not tell me when he was going out of town, wouldn't take me on a proper date because he was "too busy." He stopped calling me, would only text, barely ever answered my calls, and ditched me at two weddings. His place was pretty bare and abnormally clean; he would get mad if I was playing with my hair and a strand fell. All these things I considered weird, but I thought I loved him.

Why was I with him, you ask? He was charming. He knew all the right things to say, when to say them, how to wriggle his way back into my life each time I told myself I was done. This man made me feel safe in the chaos of life, as if nothing else mattered when we were together, and he seemed to appreciate the little things I did for him and in life in general. He was hardworking, with two or three jobs, supposedly, even allowing me to help him out once in a while just to see me when both our schedules were tight. He made just enough effort to keep me where he wanted me. No more, no less.

Then the big "get out now" signs appeared. I really started to notice his lack of belongings and that he didn't seem to keep any of the presents I would give him. "It must be downstairs," or, "They're packed away," he'd tell me. One day, I went through his room to find a t-shirt. After all, being together almost two years, you would think it's no big deal, but I came across diamond rings. Used diamond rings. Were they real? I didn't know. I didn't pick them up to find out, only lost my mind and called my best friend. "Maybe he's not ready to let go of his past. Maybe he keeps them as a reminder of his failed marriage," she tried to console me. Still, things didn't seem right. I told him I would like to talk about something and he told me, "It's probably some BS, so I'll just let it be."

What? Something was definitely fishy there. I hopped on Facebook and noticed many of his girlfriends, who he seemed close with the previous year, didn't seem to be around any longer. So, I did what any curious, hurt woman would and contacted a couple of them. I was told things such as, "That's funny, I dated him last year and broke up with him because he was engaged," and, "I deleted him a few weeks ago. I just can't believe he was this bad and acted like he was so honest. It honestly makes me sick." They told me that they had been with him in the previous year, that he got a couple women pregnant in the same timeframe, and that he may already have children that he won't own up to. I'm hearing all this while he is yelling at me via text. Apparently, one of them let him know I was in contact with her. Again, what? My mind was racing; my heart hurting. He was yelling at me for finding out the truth?

When confronted face to face, he lied his way through it, making me feel like I was crazy and it was all in my head. I started to believe it. I went along with it for a couple weeks, thinking maybe the girls were crazy; I couldn't imagine the drama he dealt with being an athlete. Until that morning came.

I was finishing breakfast next to my Nonno as I got a text that said, "Ur awesome ur a great friend ur a great person but it can never be more than that." At the same time, I get a friend request from a woman in Florida. Curious, I add her and ask if we know each other, and then I notice that we have my man in common.

She calls me and says, "He proposed in October."

"That's funny, that's when he started saying 'I love you' to me," I replied. He must not have wanted to mix us up, or maybe forgot who he was saying goodbye to that day. At this point, I was done. I couldn't even fathom all the bull I had believed and put up with for two years; staying loyal to a man who didn't know how to put anyone first but himself. I don't understand how I started to believe I was crazy, that I was making things up in my head. Clearly, it was never me; it was him playing mind games to get what he wanted.

Sometimes, we turn a blind eye to unhealthy behavior in favor of what we think is love. In reality, we should listen to our gut, pay attention to our inner voice. Mine told me not to bother with him from the start. If I would have just listened to that part of me saying, "Run!" then I wouldn't have lost two years of my life. If I would have listened to my family and friends constantly asking when they were going to meet him and informing me it was an unhealthy relationship, I could have avoided constant heartbreak. But I didn't, and now I can say that I learned a valuable lesson.

During those two years, I figured out how to cope with being in such a relationship and deciding if it was right for me. Journaling was my number one stress reliever and initial calming tool. If I was upset with something he said or did—or didn't do, in many cases—I would write poems or letters to him in my journal. Then, I'd leave the situation be for a day or two to get my head clear before deciding how to proceed. Sometimes I would skip this step and let my emotions and anger take over, but that never went well. I would get more upset because I was acting from a place of anger and pain instead of from a sound mind. Things would never get solved or go the way I planned.

My second source of coping was to talk to my mom or best friend; both of whom I trust with my life. Both had different ways of showing me that I had choices. Neither would tell me what to do or judge me, but they would guide me through my thoughts and emotions, and simply give their opinions. It was refreshing to hear honest opinions whether I liked what they had to say or not. Sometimes I disagreed, and sometimes I knew they were right, but wasn't ready to admit it yet. I knew they could see it from an outside perspective and they had more experience in the dating world than I. Many times, I chose to stick with my man. I didn't want to be the woman who didn't try hard enough or fight hard enough for him, didn't want to be the woman who left her man when he seemed to need me the most. Little did I know I'd find out how little he needed me in his life.

The final way of coping was to confront him about my feelings. Many times, after I gave myself time to calm down after an argument or something he said or did that upset me, I'd bring the issue to him. Staying calm and trying to remain positive in a negative situation was what made me realize he was only in this when things were positive. He couldn't, or didn't, want to handle me when I was upset or in need of him. Those were the times he would disappear until I had calmed down and could be nice—basically, until I pretended nothing had happened because I missed him and didn't want to stay angry. Otherwise, he would avoid speaking or acknowledging that anything upsetting had happened in the first place. Confrontation is a part of any good relationship. It's needed to sort things out, work through your differences. We never had that. It took me awhile to admit it to myself, but our relationship was anything but healthy.

The beauty of life is we get to move on. We get to continue to love, hope, and be ourselves in a world full of the good, the bad, and the ugly. Love unconditionally, with all your heart, no matter if someone hurt you. The next one won't be the same. Hope with all your being. Believe that things will be different, that you will find what you are looking for. Never give up on yourself. You are a unique individual—always be you! I learned to follow my instincts, never ignore them. We get those feelings for a reason. Our gut knows what we need more than we do. Don't ignore your inner voice.

Briane Amodeo

Born in Chicago and raised in the suburbs, Briane had a busy life with divorced parents. Growing up changing houses every other weekend took getting used to but having two houses for double the love was a wonderful thing. The encouragement, and feeling of always wanting to please, led to being a high honor student through high school while being in the color guard and on the track team, where she was a thrower.

Originally attending the University of Wisconsin—Parkside with a partial scholarship and majoring in criminal justice, Briane chose to change her life drastically and transfer to The Illinois Institute of Art—Schaumburg for photography after a year and a half. After two and a half years there, she completed her bachelor's degree in fine arts with a concentration in photography.

After stumbling through college wondering where to go in life, she never wanted to own her own company, however, less than two years later, she launched BriAmo Photography Inc. (the name coming from throwing around ideas at her internship!) BriAmo Photography is growing and Briane can see a future for herself and the budding photographers she will help over the years. She also donates her photography skills when possible.

In Briane's free time, her dog is her life, and almost her size, weighing in at 120 pounds. Spending time with her family is also a huge part of her and she gets to spend it with her cousins doing another thing she loves: water sports! She has tubed since she was around five years old, when she learned to swim, skied since she was 11, and taught herself to kneeboard in her teens. Briane has always had a love for motorcycles, obtaining a motorcycle license when she turned 18, but has never splurged on getting herself a bike. We all need a dream!

Briane Amodeo
BriAmo Photography Inc.
225 Grand Ridge Road
St. Charles, IL 60175
224-406-2325
briane.amodeo@gmail.com
www.BriAmo.com

Cathy Sirvatka

I'm Not Creative. Oh Wait… Yes I Am!

It was just a fact I had always known: I'm not creative. My mother is creative. She's an artist; an impressionist painter. Her mother was a painter as well. My older sister picked up that artistic gene too, being skillful and creative at painting, drawing, and writing. Art and visual creativity were highly regarded in my family. But as a child, I knew I wasn't creative, because my mother would set up still-life scenes for my sister and I to draw, and mine were always the worst. I always felt bad about my abilities, even though I was comparing myself to my sister who was two years older than me. But no one refuted what I believed to be true. I wasn't creative.

Ironically, I was the only one in my immediate family to go to an arts college with a creative major: photography. When you go to a creative school in a big city like Chicago, you are surrounded by people dressed in black and oozing creative genius. Of course, I compared myself to them and that gave me even greater insecurity. I assumed they were all more creative than me. And I didn't own enough black clothes.

During my last year of college, I took an advanced photography course that focused on color theory and symbolism. I loved the subject matter. The instructor (I'll call him Jay), was a tyrant. He was arrogant and rude, and blew up in class with some frequency. Though I did learn a lot from him, he should not have been a teacher.

A few weeks before the end of the semester, each student was working on their big final project. During those last weeks we still all met in class, but mostly each student would talk one-on-one with Jay about their ideas and how things were coming along. One week before the project was due, I sat down for my time with Jay, presenting my photos in which I had recreated scenes of a recurring childhood dream. My project was quite cathartic and allowed me to pour my heart and soul into the symbolism of the content using eerie imagery and deep rich colors. I don't think I ever felt more creative than I did working on this project.

To my shock, he absolutely hated it! In fact, his criticism got so loud that he involved the entire class. I cannot even tell you exactly what he said, because at that point I felt myself mentally checking out, withdrawing backward from my eyeballs. He was humiliating me to the point where other students were coaxing me to defend myself. One guy even started arguing with Jay on my behalf, but I couldn't speak up. All my strength went into not crying. My face was red, my heart was pounding, and I was as embarrassed as I had ever been in my entire life. When the carnage had finished, after about 20 minutes, I clumsily picked up my portfolio and all my pictures and left. He confirmed it loud and clear: I'm not creative.

I sobbed all the way home—big, messy, snorting, gasping sobs. I had been wounded to my core. I'm unacceptable. I'm not good enough. I'm not creative. I'm less than. All the negative assertions I believed as a child and carried into adulthood now lay bare for all to see.

The next day I called my mother to tell her what had happened. I told her how mean he was and how humiliated I felt. And her response, without missing a beat, was, "Well, you did draw bananas with a purple crayon." One might think the purple crayon was a creative choice for a 9-year-old, but Mom meant it negatively and I knew it. If I left the next pages blank you might get some idea of how I felt in that moment. I had no words. To paraphrase singer and song writer Lucinda Williams, I felt like I'd been shot and didn't fall down. "K, mom, gotta go." More sobs.

Do you believe you are not creative?

So many people tell me they are not creative. Some pronounce it with certitude. When people say this, I believe they are thinking about the typical art media: painting, drawing, writing, etc. I also think they were told this at some point in their lives.

But creativity comes in many forms and is used in every line of work. If you have solved a problem, you used creativity to do it. And the way you solved that problem was different from how someone else would have done it. The solution has your signature on it.

I believe there are two parts to creativity: *conceiving* an idea and *executing* that idea. I think the *execution* part is where people get hung up. Just because you can't maneuver a paint brush or pencil to match an image you see, either in your mind or in front of you, doesn't mean you're not creative. That's just a skill that needs to be learned and honed. And still, you may not have that kind of coordination or even the desire to make pictures. I wasn't very skilled at drawing or painting, but I loved the camera.

Back in the classroom.

After having been publicly lambasted by my discouraging instructor, I processed through all the feelings that came up; feelings of inadequacy and shame. Those feelings gave way to anger, and out of the anger came fortitude. I thought, this is MY dream (literally) that I am trying to visually communicate, and quite honestly, I think I'm doing a pretty good job of it. It's MY story to tell. And if you don't like it, well give me an F, because I'm telling it!

I reshot my entire project in that last week. I used the same concept but reworked the scenes and zhushed up the colors. And I cursed Jay through the entire process.

Then the time came for that final critique. In that last class of the semester, each student would post their images on the front board, tell the story of their project, and then the teacher would give his comments. I put my project up early in the class to get it over with. I was nauseous and angry. My mind was spinning, but I was braced for the storm. With pursed lips and one eyebrow up for attitude, I put my work on the board and tossed out just a few comments before sitting down.

Then Jay got up. I heard, "The use of these colors brings us into Cathy's dream experience. The imagery is haunting and *blah blah blah…* this work is excellent!"

What?! Wait, what? I don't get it. Had I truly improved from the darkest of nights to the brightest of lights because of a verbal beating and one week's work? Not likely. I do think my final work had improved some, but honestly, I think he realized how obnoxious and rude he had been and was making up for it. He even walked me out of the building after class. He went on about how great my project was and how he knew I had it in me, as if his chastising was the kick in the butt I needed to achieve my potential.

After receiving an A in that class (can you believe it?) and completing all my credits, I graduated with honors.

Hey! Am I creative? I think I may be. Not with a brush or pencil, but with a camera. I got A's in all of my classes. With this new information in my life, I felt my confidence growing. And all the criticism I received in all my other photography courses (all much more constructive than in Jay's class) didn't mean I wasn't creative or good. It meant I was a student who had room for improvement.

Just because someone doesn't like your work, doesn't mean it's not good.

When you think about some of the most creative people in history, not all were readily accepted. For example, Claude Monet's impressionistic style of painting was initially frowned upon and rejected by the traditional salons and critics. Popular artists of the day were painting in a realistic style, and this new technique was blurry and undesirable. Many creatives are not even artists. Albert Einstein's teachers called him lazy and said he would never amount to much; not very encouraging. But I think it took a bit of creativity to conceive the Theory of Relativity, don't you? Sometimes creativity takes you outside the box, and this will attract criticism.

Criticism comes in many forms and not all are bad. Being scathingly attacked and receiving constructive criticism are two different things. Receiving healthy criticism is one of the most important things you can do for your personal and professional growth. However, sometimes the truth is hard to hear when it's not what you are hoping for. Truth that comes in a complimentary form is easy and makes you feel accomplished and worthy. Truth about something that needs improvement is much harder to accept.

Just because someone has an opinion, doesn't make them right.

What you do in your life and business is quite naturally enmeshed with the core of who you are. Whenever you come up with a new idea, product or service, you're using your creative skills, and you are putting a piece of yourself out there for others to see. You make yourself vulnerable by pulling back the curtain on your heart just a little bit. So, when someone trounces all over your creation it is very easy to become hurt, angry, defensive, or even offensive. Maybe a part of you believes they are right. You may shrink back, thinking you don't really have anything to offer. And then maybe you hide yourself away.

The reality is, you may never run into a "Jay" in your life. I hope you don't. But you will hear criticism, both positive and negative. In fact, I challenge you to seek it out. Seriously. Not the negative, damaging, vitriolic type; but honest, constructive criticism. Seek opinions from people you know and trust to give you honest feedback in a positive manner. You never know what people will say, but remember you are hearing this information from someone you trust. Think about their comments and see if you agree. Keep in mind that just because someone offers an opinion, it doesn't mean they are right or that you should make changes. It's just information. Not everyone will like your ideas, but there are a lot of people who will. To quote another singer and song writer, Jewel, "You have to get rid of how you hope people perceive you and you just have to be willing to be perceived."

Creativity morphs.

After finishing school, I began to hear about the World Wide Web. Talk about creativity of the unusual kind! Tim Berners-Lee, a smart, hard-core computer programmer, used incredible vision and imagination to conceive and invent what would become one of the most important inventions of the 20th century. I took a class in HTML, the computer language used to create web pages, and discovered I understood it. I am by no means a programmer, but with this simple code I was amazed at the beautiful web page layouts I could create. I am creative! Now it's with a computer.

You are creative too. Don't let anyone — including yourself — tell you otherwise. Think about how you use creativity during your day. Even picking out clothes to wear for the day involves your own aesthetic choices. Start to take notice of decisions you make, ideas you come up with, or problems you solve. Could other people do what you did? Yes, probably. But the difference is, to paraphrase one more musician, you did it your way.

Cathy Sirvatka

Cathy Sirvatka has been working with small business owners to put their best foot forward on the Internet since 1999. Her working style is to get to know her clients and their businesses through one-on-one conversations. She then manifests what she has learned into a web presence that directly matches their business and attracts their ideal clients.

Prior to her web design career, Cathy earned her B.A. in Photojournalism at Columbia College in Chicago. She worked her way through school as a Word Processor at AT&T Bell Laboratories. She had become disenchanted with her new career choice and burned out on her camera by the time she graduated. It was her work at Bell Labs, however, that taught her about the World Wide Web and how to write code to make web pages.

In 1999, Cathy was laid off from Bell Labs and began her website career working for a "dot-com" firm, designing and developing websites.

In 2002, she set out on her own as a freelancer, and eventually incorporated Sirvatka Creative Services. She was also an adjunct faculty member at the College of DuPage in Glen Ellyn, Illinois for 12 years, teaching web design courses.

Cathy carries almost two decades of knowledge of the website industry and enjoys sharing that knowledge with others. She enjoys educating her clients as much or as little as they want, understanding that not everyone wants to know "how the sausage is made."

Cathy Sirvatka
Sirvatka Creative Services, Inc.
2805 Powell Court
Naperville, IL 60563
630-254-2301
cathy@sirvatka.com
www.sirvatka.com

Erin Pignatello

Mighty Me!

I often contemplate how quickly life can change. In a blink of an eye, our world can be completely turned upside down. We can go from being on top of the world to the depths of despair in just one moment.

We all face challenges. Challenges are everywhere and unavoidable. These challenges can either define us or destroy us. Thankfully, my biggest challenge was not able to take hold of me permanently. Instead, it did just the opposite; it lifted me up, changed who I am and put me on the path to become Mighty Me!

It has been years since my struggles began. Sometimes I find myself feeling normal for a few days and I almost forget that there is anything wrong with me. Then something triggers my body, a flare up occurs, and I am quickly reminded of my delicate health limitations. I am a victim of what I call "Eyes Wide Shut." I put my trust in all the wrong places and it almost cost me my life. How could I have known? No one told me. No one warned me. I guess it was something I had to learn on my own.

The summer of 2013 was the year that I had to face this challenge. It all started with a simple feeling in my heart. I was driving alone in my car when a thought came to me: "You have been blessed with good health but everything can change in a blink of an eye." As I continued to drive, I thought, *that was very strange,* but I brushed it aside and did not think about it again. Now, I know that prompting was from God, a sign of difficult yet great things to come.

The very next morning after my experience in the car, I woke up and went about my day. It wasn't until later that night that I noticed when my hair touched the side of my face it caused a weird sensation. It was starting to annoy me, but I brushed it off thinking it was nothing and would go away. A few days later, the sensation was still there and progressively getting worse. It was beginning to feel like bugs were crawling around on the right side of my face, and whenever my hair touched my skin it agitated and enhanced the feeling. I began putting my hair up in a clip to keep it from touching my face.

To make matters a little more difficult, I was leaving for California to attend my brother's wedding when the worst of it hit me and I almost could not get on the plane. The morning of my flight I woke up with my face swollen and looking like someone had repeatedly smacked me. My eyelids were especially swollen and felt like they were on fire; I could barely open them or look into the sunlight. I felt dizzy, nauseous and quite honestly, like I had been hit by a car. Despite all of this I got on the plane and headed to California.

Upon arriving, I experienced lock jaw for the first time in my life. If you have ever experienced lock jaw, then you know it can be quite terrifying and excruciatingly painful. These thirty seconds of sheer panic and pain caused days of soreness that made eating very painful. This was the beginning of my chronic lock jaw condition that reared its ugly head every time I yawned, chewed my food a certain way, or simply opened my mouth too widely. While my brother's wedding was beautiful and my time with my family precious, I spent five days in secret agony, wrought with widespread bodily pain and an overall feeling of sickness. Every room I entered felt slanted to me, as though I was walking uphill. The smell of food was bothering me and I ate very little. For the first time in my life I experienced sea sickness as we toured the Pacific Ocean for five hours in search of ocean life. My body felt like it was breaking down.

Upon arrival back home, I was experiencing intense pain and weird sensations all over my body. But the bugs, oh those stupid bugs crawling all over the right side of my face were my undoing. One morning, that horrible sensation began to travel from the right side of my face over the bridge of my nose onto the left side of my face and into my eyes. I cried until I had no tears left begging God to make it stop. I then called my mother and told her I couldn't take it anymore, that I was living in hell. My mother convinced me to call the doctor. I called the doctor and begged them to see me immediately, otherwise I might jump off the George Washington Bridge. Well, that caught their attention and the receptionist scheduled me in immediately.

I was quickly led into the Neurologist's office and she spoke to me for a while, writing down all of my symptoms. She then proceeded to do a physical neurological examination that tested my body's responses and was shocked at how poorly I responded. She immediately scheduled me for an MRI at a near imaging center and had my blood draw for evaluation.

A few days later I received a phone call from my doctor saying that the blood work came back negative for diseases like Multiple Sclerosis, Lupus, Lyme Disease and cancer; however, they spotted multiple lesions on my brain. Unfortunately, it was inconclusive as to why, or what was causing the lesions and my symptoms. This was the beginning of a long line of doctors who told me, "I don't know what is wrong with you, but we will get to the bottom of it." I can assure you, no doctor ever got to the bottom of it. Instead I was put on many different medications, laughed at, embarrassed, humiliated, and one doctor even told me to see a psychiatrist because I was making my symptoms up.

My husband began researching my symptoms and discovered something called Gluten Ataxia. This is a condition where gluten causes all kinds of neurological symptoms and can actually cause lesions on the brain. He suggested that I go gluten free. Against my neurologist's advice, I took my husband's advice and immediately took gluten out of my diet. Within three days I noticed a significant decrease in the feelings on my face and was actually able to release my hair from the clip I pulled it up with. I thought that I had found the problem and that I would begin to heal. Unfortunately, this was not the case. While the feelings of bugs crawling on my face was beginning to subside, I still felt them come and go multiple times throughout the day and night.

Just when I thought I was getting my symptoms somewhat manageable

I began to develop electrical feelings in the front of my brain. It was as though static electricity was occurring in my brain and coming out through my eyelashes. This left my entire face feeling staticky and sent me into a full blown panic attack. The only thing that would help me was getting into the shower and letting water hit my face, after which I would go to sleep in order to hide from the torture I was feeling.

I spent a better part of three years going doctor to doctor, being handed one medication after another and enduring one procedure after another. With every day that passed, I felt as though I was losing a piece of me as depression, anxiety and medications took hold of me. After three years of searching, my folder containing all of my medical records was five inches thick. Five inches, yet, nothing. With each doctor that failed to properly diagnose me, I would move on to the next. I endured many different procedures including blood work, MRI's, X-rays, Ultrasounds, Somatosensory Evoked Potential Tests of my eyes and upper and lower extremities (this is where they hook up wires and send electrical stimulus through electrodes which determine the amount of time it takes for the current to travel along the nerves to my brain), and a lumbar puncture followed by the worst headache that I could ever imagine. This headache left me immobile for days. I was unable to stand up, sit up, or open my eyes without feeling like my head was going to explode, followed by nausea. I had no choice but to go back into the hospital for another procedure called an Epidural Blood Patch. This surgical procedure is performed to treat headaches and leaks of cerebrospinal fluid. Its sole purpose is to patch the hole in the dura, which makes the headache go away. The patient is awake during the procedure and has to lie on their belly while blood is extracted from a vein in the arm and quickly injected into the epidural space (same location as the lumbar puncture). Patients usually experience relief immediately. This was not the case for me. It took another two days for the blood patch to take effect. I was hours away from having to endure another Epidural Blood Patch when relief finally washed over my brain.

One evening as I lay in bed crying to my husband, I told him I did not think I could live the rest of my life like this. He simply stated, "You may not have a choice." That was my "aha" moment. Being told that I had no choice changed everything for me, because we always have choices. There is always a way out. It was time for me to dig deep, to rely on myself and God to figure this out. I told my husband, "No way. I will not live the rest of my life like this and if doctors cannot figure this out, I will."

I began intense research and documenting my symptoms. I needed to see when they happened, what I was around, what I was eating and what symptoms I felt at that moment. After weeks of observation, I discovered I had an airborne, touch and ingestible sensitivity to gluten. I continued to investigate further into my foods and began discovering exactly what was in the foods I had been eating. I was shocked and horrified. Chemicals were in all of the foods that I was eating. I also discovered that my foods were genetically modified, therefore losing their pure nutrients.

I immediately started a gluten-, soy-, and dairy-free diet that consisted of organic foods. The feelings of bugs and static electricity began to subside. Unfortunately, my anxiety and panic attacks were still present. I was in desperate need of something besides medication to help my body, mind, and heart heal from what I had endured the past three years.

I prayed to God, asking Him to guide me to find the healing power that I so desperately needed. I attended a gluten-free convention in Phoenix, Arizona, with my niece. As soon as we walked through the doors there was a sign showing classes that were occurring throughout the day. The doTERRA Essential Oils class stood out above all the rest and I told my niece to make sure that we went to that class. During the class, I was educated on the amazing uses of essential oils. Peppermint essential oil was passed around for everyone to smell. When I smelled that bottle of precious oil, it was like my brain instantly responded and woke up. My brain screamed for more. I wanted to drink the oil in and let my brain succumb to it. I had never experienced anything like it before. After the class, I immediately proceeded to the doTERRA booth where

I experimented with many different oils and felt a strong pull toward them all. I left that evening with a box of three essential oils (lavender, peppermint, and lemon) and a mentor to help train me with their many different uses. The plane ride home was bittersweet as I read materials about these precious oils. My heart was full of God's love. I knew He sent me to that place, where healing could finally begin.

I dove into the world of holistic healing headfirst, never stopping, never looking back. I ate, drank, breathed, and bathed in my oils. Peppermint helped relaxed the feeling of bugs crawling on my face. It was as though my brain was taking a deep sigh of relief and spreading that relief like a blanket over my face, eyes and body. I no longer needed the medication that I had been taking for the nerve damage on my face. Lavender essential oil helped to keep me calm and soon my panic attacks completely subsided and I no longer needed my antianxiety medication. I was beginning to feel joy again. Frankincense was used to help alleviate the electrical feeling that I felt in the front of my brain. I was healing quicker than I ever thought possible. Through the good grace of God, I had found His precious gifts from Earth that bring me peace and good health every day of my life.

After two years of daily use of doTERRA Essential Oils, I have become a new me, a Mighty Me! I live an organic lifestyle, free of the chemicals and toxins that once poisoned my body. I also started my own doTERRA Essential Oils business where I get to share my story with those who will hear, spreading the good news that there is hope, there is peace, there is healing when you let God's gifts into your heart, your home, and your life. Who am I? What is my real purpose? My purpose is to rise above my challenges to become a healthier, happier, and wiser me. I faced my fears, but above all I learned to trust in me, and I found victory!

This story is dedicated to my mom, who recently passed after thirteen years of battling Frontal Lobe Dementia. Thank you for sticking by my side and trying your hardest to be my advocate. I love you!

Erin Pignatiello

Growing up, family was a constant and stable part of Erin's life. Her strong desire to be a mother was born out of her family ties and the constant love that surrounded her. Erin was raised and still lives in the state of New Jersey. She has lived in the same small town for most of her life. In this small town, Erin met her future husband at the age of nine. They began dating at age sixteen and married at age twenty-five. A mother of three children, two girls and one boy, Erin was living the life she dreamed of having as a stay at home mom.

Erin worked for eleven years in various positions within her family owned business. She also worked as an ABA Therapist for children on the Autism spectrum. During this time, Erin was working on a college degree in Elementary Special Education. Erin is currently completing her bachelor of science in elementary education and special education at Grand Canyon University.

The summer of 2013 was a turning point for Erin's health. She developed neurological symptoms that caused mental, physical and emotional pain. Erin spent two years going doctor to doctor, procedure to procedure, in search of a doctor and cure. Unfortunately, that doctor was never found. Erin was left to discover her condition and treatment on her own. This is when she became her own "Mighty Me".

In November 2016, Erin found relief from the use of doTERRA's peppermint essential oil. This gift from God brought immediate relief and as a result, Erin dove into the world of essential oils and holistic living. Erin started her own business as a trained Wellness Advocate for doTERRA International and shares her story of personal triumph over sickness as she educates others about the use of essential oils.

Erin Pignatiello
DoOilsDoterra
16 Sunnyside Avenue
Dumont, NJ 07628
201-658-9420
dooilsdoterra@gmail.com
www.mydoterra.com/erinpignatiello

Monique Horb

Get Up and Get Dressed

My marriage was in the pits. I put on a mask. It was a mask that I suspect many of us wear: the mask of protection, the mask that will allow us to keep putting one foot in front of the other without being honest with ourselves. If I had been honest, I would have fallen apart. I would have admitted that I needed help and didn't have the answer to this big, ugly problem. People would see my failure. I wasn't willing to do it.

This isn't what I signed up for. How could this life be mine? Why aren't you listening to me, answering my prayers? I questioned God again and again. Over and over I replayed in my mind where I was and how I got there. I thought, since I had made the right decisions and followed the rules and prayed, God would answer all my prayers with the answers that I wanted. I thought life would be easy. A great marriage, thriving at work, mission trips, vacations… Living our dream.

My husband was working close to 100 hours a week trying to save our business, which was in a tailspin. His "girlfriend" (as I liked to call his business) was taking all of his time, and I felt like a married single mom. I was lonely, miserable, and angry. I didn't even know that this was a red flag. I just wanted my husband to choose me. To love me. What did I need to do to get his attention? Why wasn't I good enough for him?

I continued to pretend to my friends that things were fine, until I couldn't pretend anymore. So, then I just withdrew from my friends. I did, however, continue to go to a Bible study class. But even then, I attended at a church I had attended previously, because I didn't want people to know that my world, my marriage, was falling apart. I was trying to protect my husband. I didn't want anyone to know, I didn't want to be judged, and I didn't want to ask for help.

I attended this class for several months, until I finally broke down and cried all over a table. I shared how I wanted to "cross the solid yellow line." I shared that, as I was driving down the two-lane highway in our town, I kept thinking, *If I could just cross the median into the opposite lane of traffic, the next semi-truck could end this.* End the sadness, disappointment, and frustration. But who would take care of my children if I did that?

I had been using so much energy to live day by day that I hadn't even realized that I was losing myself. All I could see in my mind's eye was a visual of water swirling down the drain of a bathtub. I felt like my life was swirling faster and faster down the drain with nobody to grab onto. I had pulled away from all my friendships, which allowed me to hide the reality of my situation. I was encouraged by the women in the group to find a counselor and talk to my doctor.

My husband did file bankruptcy and was miserable with himself. I believe he felt like a failure and struggled with his own questions about what to do. At this time we had three children, and I felt very alone, exhausted, and overwhelmed. I became depressed and finally sought some help from my doctor.

I also had a friend who cornered me. She told me that she knew something was wrong, and she wasn't leaving until she knew what was going on. I finally shared how miserable everything was, and she listened. She didn't try to fix it; she just listened. She approached my husband and myself separately and suggested that we go to a Crisis Marriage counseling week in Georgia. I was willing to try, but didn't think that my husband would ever agree to it because he was so focused on his business. I knew that this would be the last-ditch effort to save our marriage. My husband finally agreed to go.

The Crisis Marriage counseling week was pivotal, not only in my marriage, but in who I am. The counseling focused on the idea of self-care. I felt like I was listening to a foreign language. What did "self-care" even mean? What were they talking about? I learned that if I didn't care for myself, I wouldn't be able to care for my family and my marriage the way I needed to.

It took several months to really learn what self-care looked like and why it was so important in my life. Once I learned the value of caring for myself, I began my ascent to self-worth. I began to take care of myself and get healthier.

A year after we were in counseling, my husband and I were on an airplane to Ukraine to complete the process of adoption. Three years prior to this, we had started the adoption process and now it was time to complete it. Doors had kept shutting, as our lives were in chaos. Now, the doors were open, and we were on the way to adopting children.

I was often asked why we were adopting, since we already had three children. My answer was simple: the Lord had pointed us in that direction and opened the doors when we were ready. I knew that it didn't make sense, and even had people tell us that we had no business adopting since we were rebuilding our marriage. The only answer I had for them was the same: He told us to. So, we came home with three children; not the two that we had anticipated. Our family of five became eight, and three kids became six. The overwhelm of a bigger family and all that was involved was a challenge!

I became a problem solver. I had to learn out how to manage a blended family. I had to find solutions to everyday problems: how to manage schedules, meals, time, conflicts, and our household. This was my challenge, and I had no idea how to do any of it.

Two years after we adopted our children, one of them had an extremely rare medical condition which resulted in brain surgery. After the procedure, we were told that he would have died if it hadn't been caught in time. I felt like I had been kicked in the stomach. By God's grace and with talented medical care, he recovered well. We were told that there was a 0.67% chance that this would ever happen again. We felt so relieved to hear this.

Eleven months later, my son began having headaches and got very sick. My husband looked at me and said, "I think it's his head." My stomach sank, and fear gripped my heart. But I put on my "big girl hat" and went to work, making phone calls to his physicians and getting the proper tests done. Twelve months later he was on the operating table again. I prayed that God would save my son a second time.

This time the recovery was not easy. In fact, it took months for him to feel normal again. This placed an even greater strain on me than the first time, because of the additional medical care. Juggling our family's schedule and my son's health care was a full-time job.

I have had many people ask me, "How do you do it? It seems like you always have *something*." My response has been, "I get up and get dressed!" This was the only way that I knew how to keep going.

I also had to learn how to act instead of reacting. This has been by far my biggest challenge. When you choose to act, you make a conscious decision about what you will do and say. When you react, you respond with emotion first. I realized that, until I chose to walk away from the bitterness and anger I felt about all the things that I thought were unfair in my life, I would stay stuck in negative belief about myself.

As I continued to grow, I learned that all I needed to do was show up. Show up in my marriage, show up for my kids. Show up even when I didn't know what to do next. Being a problem solver, I began to show up and find the answers. Showing up can be hard, but it is when the work can happen.

It was at this point in my life that I began to see my purpose. I knew that I was good at organizing; I had somehow been able to keep our busy family of eight fed, clothed, and alive. I figured since I could organize our home for eight people as well as schedules and activities, I could surely help other people organize their lives. So, I hung out my shingle and got to work!

I began to help overwhelmed women organize, and discovered that I was really good at it! I knew that if I could help them get their homes organized, they wouldn't feel so frustrated and would be able to feel better about themselves. As I continued helping people, I discovered that time management is also a big part of organizing a home. I began to help people get their paper organized, and with this, they were able to become more productive and feel empowered. I encouraged them and cheered them on. I told them I knew they could do it... and they did!

I chose to embrace my faith, and began to believe that I am chosen by God and that I have value. As a result I gained more confidence, and I began to help women get out from under the chaos of their lives, and from feelings of being defeated and overwhelmed. To empower women who struggle with negative beliefs about themselves and their circumstances has become my passion and purpose.

I choose to live my life on purpose. I want to encourage women to take off the mask and ask for help. Everyone has something they are struggling with. However, living behind the mask will keep you from moving forward and embracing change.

Why do we worry so much about what others think about us? If we choose to take our masks off, and we're vulnerable, we can embrace and encourage others who might have the same feelings or who have had similar situations. This is when we discover what we are made to do.

This is how we learn how to move forward: by sharing our struggles and leaning on one another. When we share our burdens, we can be open to hear solutions, encouragement and hope. While taking off the mask doesn't mean that life is going to be easy, it does gives us a better chance to change our lives and live our purposes. Encouraging those around us by sharing our stories helps us to move forward. We can then reach back a hand and help someone who is struggling in the space that we once were. Life isn't supposed to be lived alone, but with others, so that we can cheer each other along.

I believe the verse that states, "I can do all things through Christ who strengthens me." (Philippians 4:13). Faith does not make things easy; it makes things possible. I want to encourage you to take a step of faith, ask for help, and choose to live. I will be here cheering you on!

Monique Horb

Monique Horb has a passion for helping women who are busy, tired, and overwhelmed. She does this by organizing homes and paper piles so that women can be more productive, have time and energy to live their purpose, and live the life they want. She loves to say, *Life Is Easier Organized!*

She began her business, Organizing Your Chaos, after experiencing depression, bankruptcy, adoption, marriage and medical crisis. These things were out of her control, and her home was falling apart. Through twists and turns, she learned that with an organized home she was able to manage.

Monique was raised in southwest Michigan and graduated from Taylor University, a Christian college in Indiana, with a BA in Sociology & Psychology. She met her husband through a friend while working at Spring Hill Camps in Michigan. They have been married for twenty-five years and have six children, two dogs and a cat. Her life experiences have pushed her out of her comfort zone and shaped the business that she created.

She loves to help women who struggle to get their homes organized. She knows that the simple (yet difficult) act of getting your home organized gives hope. Hope propels us forward, gives confidence, and allows changes to happen. This can change your life.

When asked, "How do you do it?" she responds, "I get up and get dressed."

She believes that being willing to take off the mask, ask for help and work hard, alongside a faith in God, has changed her life. She continues to help women change their lives, and shares that we are all better when we are in community together.

Monique Horb
Organizing Your Chaos
2654 Calaveras Drive
Valparaiso, IN 46385
219-595-2548
Monique@OrganizingYourChaos.com
www.OrganizingYourChaos.com

Hope Restored® A Marriage Intensive Experience
www.HopeRestored.FocusOnTheFamily.com

Dr. Sylvia Hood Washington CLT-LANA

Hidden Healer

When I was sitting at my desk in the late 1980s as one of NASA's first African American journeyman systems engineers in the Midwest, becoming a nationally certified lymphatic clinician was never my intention or my dream. Sudden and abnormally intense swelling of my legs and feet, to twice their size in literally one day, would eventually change my life and the lives of my family and patients.

On that sunny afternoon in 1987, I felt emotionally exhausted and betrayed when I looked down at my inexplicably puffy legs and engorged feet. They were screaming against my high-end sheer stockings and through my power pumps. I knew deep down inside that this was not normal swelling, because it came on suddenly and I didn't feel any pain.

Prior to that moment I was content and dressed for success. I had received a Society of Women's Engineering/NASA scholarship to attend graduate school, and had just graduated with my Master of Science in Systems and Controls Engineering. I was finally feeling confident and secure because I had landed my dream job as a NASA engineer.

The day my legs swelled at NASA was a day packed with hours and hours of boring and repetitive meetings with other research engineers and scientists working on the planned United States Space Station's power system. I was usually the only woman and the only African American engineer in a room with dozens of men. I had been hired a few months earlier for my documented expertise in mathematical modelling and computer simulation of space power systems. I had gained this expertise through a rigorous and hostile two-year Master of Science degree program from the Case Institute of Technology at Case Western Reserve University in Cleveland, Ohio. My thesis was 250 pages long, more than five times the length of the average Master's thesis for my male counterparts. My thesis advisor told me after my defense that the department (all male engineers) had intentionally put me through almost inhuman paces because I was going to become the first African American woman to ever graduate with this degree in the 150-year history of the University. According to my advisor, they wanted to make sure that I would never be an Affirmative Action hire.

Sexual harassment and outright discrimination against women were blatant in the 1980s because women were still just beginning to break barriers in the workforce. Yes, even as a second generation "Hidden Figure" the barriers for African American female engineers, scientists and mathematicians were still high and often inhospitable.[1] A common joke openly told in almost every engineering company was, "What is the difference between garbage and a female engineer? Garbage gets taken out once a week!"

During this era, many women dropped out of engineering and science programs because of the hostility and harassment they faced; not only in the classrooms and on the job, but also in their own families and communities. I became an engineer and scientist despite aggressive efforts by teachers, professors, family members and friends to make me choose one of the more stereotypical careers that they felt were appropriate for women. Many female engineers, including me, were asked by male relatives if their next goal was to become a "man." Political correctness did not exist in those so-called times of civil rights gains and womens' liberation. Our goal as female engineers was to be fully women, fully engaged and on top of the scientific and technological challenges presented to us.

Female engineers and scientists wanted to be feminine but dared not appear weak or frail in the workforce because of persistent stereotypes about

---

1   www.barnesandnoble.com/w/summary-and-analysis-of-hidden-figures-worth-books/1125305964

the "weaker sex". Like many of my fellow female engineers and scientists, I came to work and sat through hours of meetings with premenstrual cramps, complicated pregnancies, migraines and sick children. Most of our male colleagues did not have to deal with these issues because they were either single or had wives at home who held down the fort. We also faced tension between ourselves and the clerical support staff, who were also women but were only used to working for men.

The business attire for female engineers included make-up as well as clothing. Mary Kay cosmetics was a God-send to working women, then and now.[2] Like many professional women, I did not have the time to commute to work, work up to 12 hours per day, manage a home with children and spouse, and find time to get to a department store to buy high quality cosmetics. Attending a Mary Kay cosmetics party was functional and was also a space where I got to have fun being with other women.

Eventually I became a Mary Kay Team Leader, winning my first car in less than nine months with the support of a team of female engineers from NASA. My experience with Mary Kay helped me to be the type of clinician/ healer that I am today. I was a better engineer and a better clinician because I was taught by Mary Kay how to be attentively committed, aware of others' needs, and dedicated to helping others.

Being physically fit was crucial to being in the professional game at work. To be suddenly ill, without reasoning and without a clear way to control or stop the progression of the disease, was a spiritual, mental and physical watershed moment. I had been ill every year of my life from birth, but the swollen legs was a disabling new hurdle.

After many exams and imaging tests to see if I had broken my legs or had a Deep Vein Thrombosis, I was told by the doctors at the University Hospital in Cleveland, Ohio in 1987 that I had lymphedema. The best definition for lymphedema that I have come across belongs to the Lymphatic Education

2 www.marykay.com/en-us/about-mary-kay/our-commitment

Research Network: "Lymphedema is a chronic lymphatic disease that results in disfiguring swelling in one or more parts of the body. It can be hereditary (Primary Lymphedema) or it can occur after a surgical procedure, infection, radiation or other physical trauma (Secondary Lymphedema)."[i] I was told by this first group of doctors that my life would change, that I had to resign myself to wearing compression socks every day and adjust my wardrobe to accommodate for this incurable illness. The swelling eventually moved to my arms and hand after the birth of my first child. In 1990 I was formally diagnosed with lymphedema by the famous Cleveland Clinic, following a traumatic pregnancy which led to an abnormal weight gain of 70 lbs. and medical issues that were tied to the disease.

God Does Not Close a Door Without Opening a Window

I wanted to become an engineer because I had discovered my love for mathematics, physics and science as a young girl in Cleveland, Ohio in the 1960s. I had spent half of my childhood being ill, at home and reading books because there was nothing else to do. My parents came from Alabama farms in the 1940s during the Great Migration period for African Americans fleeing the South and looking for greater social freedom and economic opportunity. My mother (a nurse) had eight children in eleven years. I was the youngest, and she hit the jackpot when I was born.

When I was born, I developed a *Staphylococcus* (bacterial) infection in the hospital and was not allowed to come home for weeks. My bouts with infections did not end there. I was always coming down with infections of all types throughout my life. Every year I would come down with the flu or a cold several times a year, and each bout would last for months. My mother was told by physicians that I had been born with **a weak immune system** and that I would never be able to stay well like other children. Neither she nor I was told in my early childhood that this poor immune system was a direct result of my having Primary Lymphedema. "The lymphatic system is part of the **immune**

---

i   www.home.liebertpub.com/publications/environmental-justice/259/for-authors

system. It fulfills the function of **'immune trafficking,'** the process whereby infection-fighting cells can be mobilized in the body where needed. When the lymphatic system is compromised by surgery, trauma, or from birth, the body is prone to recurrent infection."[3]

I feel blessed that my Mom and my Dad (a licensed welder) were people of faith and entrepreneurs who ran a successful restaurant and catering business while also working full time. My parents provided me with a strong work ethic and a strong faith in God. They also taught me that I should never give up on my dreams, and that with faith my life would be meaningful. Coming from the segregated Jim Crow South, they taught all their children about the critical importance of education in making dreams come true. I was fortunate to be raised by parents who taught me never to feel sorry for myself. I was so physically pathetic as a child that I had to argue with my parents to convince them to let me go away to college. I had a weak body but a strong mind. I was given an intellectual gift that was identified by my teachers when I was in elementary school. I could learn most things on my own, and had to, because I missed so many days at school from illnesses.

When I became a college student, I could not tell my parents that I had been coming down with an infection or the flu every semester during my four years. By the time I left college I could count on having an annual bout of flu along with pneumonia. Antibiotics and prescription medications provided me with temporary breaks from my physical battles. I trudged along and studied hard and made it through college as a science major, completing all of the requirements to attend medical school. I chose not to go to medical school because I still wanted to be an engineer and I didn't want to struggle physically for another four years in school.

I took a position right after college, in 1980, as an environmental chemist and then environmental engineer with the Cleveland Electric Illuminating Company. My health, however, grew worse every year for almost 20 years when I began to work and commute by car two to four hours per day.

3 www.lymphaticnetwork.org/living-with-lymphedema/lymphedema

Using green healing modalities according to my physicians in 1997 was the best route for me to reclaim my health. By then they had found out that I was allergic to dozens of foods and everyday substances that we encounter in our environment, like: newspapers (because of soy-based inks), automobile exhaust, new carpeting, curtains, lettuce, rice, milk, most fruits, mold and pollen, to name only a few. This assessment came after 38 years of constantly being ill; first as an infant, and then as a Full Professor of Physical Sciences and Chemistry, and after having worked for almost 15 years in the power industry as an environmental chemist and environmental control systems engineer. My personal AHA moment for the impact of pollution on my body came between 1998–2000, when I found myself working on campus during the construction of a new science center. Most of the work protocols being used during the construction violated OSHA and EPA regulations, including painting indoors during the day without proper ventilation.

This was also when one of my doctors declared that I had *Multiple Chemical Sensitivity*. It was the best conclusion they could come up with, given my reactivity to almost everything in my environment...but they were wrong! My doctors in Illinois did not read my medical records, and they did not understand that all of these reactions were tied to my compromised **immune** system. I was always going to become ill and more sensitive to the environment because I had Primary Lymphedema.[4]

Illinois physicians eventually concluded that I could not take annual flu shots and that I was allergic to most of the vitamins and supplements on the market. My physicians continued to urge me to help them find a way to heal naturally. My initial set of treating physicians and I eventually agreed that I should also learn how to use yoga to support my endocrine system and my digestive/elimination systems. We also decided I should use naturopathy to help me with nutritional choices, and natural detoxification to release chemicals that my body had absorbed on the job and in my day-to-day surroundings. All of this led me to becoming a naturopathic doctor focused on using aromatherapy,

4   www.medlineplus.gov/lymphaticdiseases.html

nutrition, reflexology and acupressure to heal myself.

Unfortunately, neither the physicians in 1987, 1990 or in the late 1990s provided me with support or explicit instruction for treating my primary lymphedema. Fortunately or divinely, I was drawn to healing techniques for the lymphatic system in all of my training as a naturopathic doctor and alternative health practitioner because I understood that it was tied to my compromised immune system. I truly believe that it was Divine intervention that kept pushing me or redirecting my focus to studying, researching and then healing people with lymphatic disorders. My STEM PhD in the History of Science, Technology, Medicine and the Environment suddenly changed from a history of electricity to a history of people with compromised health and immunity who lived in highly polluted environments (even as my own lymphatic system was shutting down as a chemistry professor).

Ultimately, my dissertation was developed into two highly esteemed books and several book chapters between 2006 and 2011: *Packing Them In* and *Echoes from the Poisoned Well*. I then began my career as a sought-after public speaker on environmental health disparities, eventually becoming an invited presenter at Yale University, Northwestern, Amherst and Duke Universities. Looking back, it is clear that all of these discussions and publications were histories about people and communities whose lymphatic systems were overloaded because of pollution.[5i]

In 2016 I felt called to not just talk about environmental health problems, but to offer green healing clinics with all of my public speaking engagements. I wanted to heal the lymphatic systems of people from environmental justice communities. The participants' responses from the clinics were so moving that they finally convinced me to open myself up to becoming a full-time lymphatic therapist. In the fall of 2017 I received training from the Klose Training Institute in Complete Decongestive Therapy (CDT), and within six months I became an internationally Certified Lymphatic Therapist by the Lymphology

---

5   www.amazon.com/Packing-Them-Sylvia-Hood-Washington/dp/1532026153;
www.amazon.com/Echoes-Poisoned-Well-Environmental-Injustice/dp/0739114328/

Association of North America (CLT-LANA).[6] It was an amazing experience to be trained first hand by Guenter Klose,[7] the founder and Executive Director of Klose Training & Consulting, LLC. "His work with lymphedema patients in the United States was instrumental in establishing the field of lymphedema training and therapy throughout the nation."[8]

Identifying the Needs

"Up to 10 million Americans, and hundreds of millions worldwide, suffer from lymphedema and lymphatic diseases. More people suffer from these diseases in the United States than suffer from Multiple Sclerosis, Muscular Dystrophy, ALS, Parkinson's disease, and AIDS—combined. The lymphatic system plays a role in AIDS, diabetes, heart disease, rheumatoid arthritis, lupus, and cancer metastasis. You can be born with the disease (primary) or you acquire the disease (secondary) from injury, infection, surgery or cancer.

100% of those treated for neck and head cancer will develop the disease. Physical trauma is a major cause of lymphatic disease among our wounded veterans.[9]

Hidden Healer: Serving the Needs of Others

After finally understanding the disease that I had been struggling with all of my life, along with my experiences with the green healing clinics, I decided that I wanted to meet the needs of the underserved lymphatic community. In 2017 I converted my L.E.E.D sustainability center into a dedicated lymphatic wellness clinic.[10] [ii] I am currently the only CLT-LANA therapist operating outside of a hospital in Illinois. I also use green complementary and alternative medicine to support lymphatic patients and environmentally sensitive populations (e.g. those with asthma, bronchitis, lupus and COPD). To support

6   www.clt-lana.org
7   www.en.wikipedia.org/wiki/Guenter_Klose
8   IBID.
9   www.lymphaticnetwork.org/living-with-lymphedema/lymphedema-and-lymphatic-diseases-affect-millions-and-concern-us-all
10   www.sylviahoodwashington.com; www.provider.kareo.com/natural-paths-for-lymphatic-wellness; www.massagebook.com/Aurora~Massage~natural-paths-for-lymphatic-wellness
ii   www.en.wikipedia.org/wiki/Leadership_in_Energy_and_Environmental_Design

this community. I also became a certified compression fitter and authorized dealer for the major lymphatic compression companies: Jobst, Juzo, Medi and Sigvaris.[11]

My services offered at the clinic include Manual Lymphatic Drainage, Complete Decongestive Therapy, Lymphatic Energy Drainage, Lymphatic Yoga, Reflexology Lymphatic Drainage, and Naturopathic Coaching and Counseling. [12]As a formally trained Doula I also support pregnant and postpartum moms experiencing pain and swelling.

My training as a Systems and Controls Engineer truly was not wasted. The lymphatic system is a complex system and its control (through therapy and compression garments) is unique to each patient. That day of swelling in 1987 revealed my true calling. I now engineer the best ways to promote lymphatic healing for all my clients.

---

11   www.sylviahoodwashington.com;
www.provider.kareo.com/natural-paths-for-lymphatic-wellness
12   www.massagebook.com/Aurora~Massage~natural-paths-for-lymphatic-wellness

Dr. Sylvia Hood Washington CLT-LANA

Sylvia Hood Washington, PhD, ND, MPH, CLT-LANA, BCTMB, HTCP, RYT-500, is an interdisciplinary trained and Board-Certified Lymphatic Therapist. Born with congenital lymphedema, she is dedicated to working with patients suffering from lymphedema, lipedema, chronic venous insufficiency, and those with compromised immune systems suffering from diseases like Lupus, Rheumatoid Arthritis and Diabetes.

Dr. Washington is a formally trained epidemiologist (MPH), a Healing Touch Certified Practitioner (HTCP). a formally trained Naturopath with a Doctorate in Naturopathy, and a Certified Lymphatic Therapist through the Lymphology Association of North America (CLT-LANA). She also uses green complementary and alternative medicine to support environmentally sensitive populations. Dr. Washington has been certified through the National Board Certification for Therapeutic Massage and Bodywork (NCTMB) and is a nationally registered yoga instructor (500 RYT).

She offers services in Manual Lymphatic Drainage (MLD-Vodder) and Complete Decongestive Therapy, Lymphatic Energy Drainage, Reflexology Lymphatic Drainage, Lymphatic Yoga and Lymphatic Breath-work, and Naturopathic Coaching and Counseling. As a formally trained Prenatal and Postpartum Doula, Dr. Sylvia offers prenatal and postnatal massage (BCTMB, LMT) for moms experiencing pain, edema and congestion and swelling.

Dr. Sylvia is the editor in chief of the international environmental health journal Environmental Justice (Mary Ann Liebert Publishers). A former Research Associate Professor at the University of Illinois at Chicago, she is the published author of two books on environmental health disparities and over a dozen articles and chapters focused on the impacts of environmental pollution and climate change on public health. A highly regarded public speaker, she has been featured on both public radio (WBEZ) and public TV (WTTW).

A former award-winning journeyman Electronic Systems and Controls Engineer from NASA, Dr. Sylvia operates out of an environmentally healthy, registered LEED Gold building, The Green Buddha Sustainability Center.

Dr. Sylvia Hood Washington CLT-LANA
Natural Paths for Lymphatic Wellness
205 W Galena Blvd
Aurora, IL 60506
630-896-8321
drsylvia@np4lymphaticwellness.com
www.SylviaHoodWashington.com

Lisa Oddo

Striving for Unconditional Love in a Conditional World

For years, I have had my Bible opened to I Corinthians 13 on a pulpit table in front of my fireplace. It has started many conversations with people who have visited my home. What warms my heart is that my youngest niece has been curious upon each visit. She stands there reading it as if each time is her first, reading aloud with curiosity and excitement in her voice. Often this sparks questions from her wise, curious mind.

"The greatest of these is Love. "It comes from I Corinthians 13:13. To preface this, the first verses of the chapter describe the attributes of love specifically. It says, (1) "If I could speak the languages of earth and of angels but didn't love others, I would only be a noisy gong or clanging symbol. (2) If I had the gift of prophecy and if I could understand all of God's secret plans and possessed all knowledge, and if I had such faith that I could move mountains but did not love others (3) If I gave everything I have to the poor and even sacrifice my body, I could boast about it, but if I didn't love others, I would have gained nothing. (4) Love is patient and kind, Love is not jealous or boastful or proud (5) or rude. It does not demand its own way. It is not irritable, and it keeps no records of being wronged. (6) It does not rejoice about injustice but rejoices whenever the truth wins out. (7) Love never gives up, never loses faith, is always hopeful, and endures through every circumstance. (8) Prophecy and speaking in unknown languages and special knowledge will become useless. But love will last forever! (9) Now our knowledge is partial and incomplete and even the gift of prophecy reveals only part of the whole picture! (10) But when the time of perfection comes, these partial things will become useless. (11) When I was a child, I spoke and thought and reasoned as a child. But when I grew up, I put away childish things. (12) Now we see things imperfectly, like puzzling reflections in a mirror, but then we will be everything completely. (13) Three things will last forever - "Faith, Hope, and Love and the greatest of these is love." My Bible is open to these pages for a constant reminder about unconditional love. It is given in a patient, kind way, not for accolades or in expectation of it to be given in return. I believe it is our human nature to want love, time, and effort reciprocated. Sometimes what we offer is like a contingency plan based on what someone gave us first. This kind of love is based on conditions. Unconditional love stays constant, and has nothing to do with our behavior. God loves us all the time even though we make mistakes every day. He doesn't shut that love off or deny us. Could you imagine loving people all the time, in the same capacity, no matter what? That would be truly amazing!

Our actions are meaningless if they aren't done out of love for others. Verses 4-8 talk about the sacrifices of love and its characteristics which are and from God. We get our love from God. Jesus was our living example of how love is given unconditionally. His ultimate gift of love was sending His son to earth to eventually take every persons' sins with him to the cross. While he was here, Jesus was the perfect mentor of how to show love. He lived simply, never had a place to call home, and never fully had the support of an earthly family, yet everything he said and did was from the love He has for us. He had so little but gave His greatest gift, which is love. From others, He experienced love and hate, obedience and disobedience, greed, illness, and was even tempted by Satan himself when alone in the wilderness. He lived as a man who went through many, if not more challenges, yet His love never wavered or changed. I feel that when we are in need the most, it's easy to falter, making mistakes that, at the time, seemed right for us. We sometimes look for love in all the wrong people, but we can still love them. In fact, the Bible tells us in Luke 6:27

that we are to love our enemies and do good to those who hate us. Positive, gentle treatment and conversation both go a very long way. It helps to soften the hardest of hearts. This can seem impossible, but we need to remember the love that Christ had for us while we were still sinners. This means we were born sinners and remain sinners, but He loves us so much. He forgives our mistakes and loves us without conditions. If we remember the love God has to offer, and the love we learned from our parents, we will be able to come out of the pit of darkness easier. Christ also felt pain, suffering, and death too. He was sent to lead, teach, mentor, be a friend, heal the sick, and prove that God is our heavenly Father. All of this is done out of His love for us. We can use His example to lead, teach, mentor, and befriend others. Sometimes all a person needs is your time, effort, skill, or friendship.

Our love tends to be conditional, based on loyalty, trust, commitment, and faithfulness. Feelings change quickly when we feel wronged, betrayed, alone, lonely, or when communication slows or seems to cease. Grudges and hurt feelings keep us from fully loving and forgiving others, as well as forgiving ourselves when we mess up. We are limited by a sinful, negative nature and can fall short intentionally, which seems evil, spiteful, and selfish. For the most part, however, we make these mistakes unknowingly. We don't know what our futures hold and we only have pieces of the puzzle, not the picture in its entirety. This is where faith and hope come in. Faith is believing in something we cannot necessarily see with our human eyes. There is something bigger and more powerful than us.

It is our spiritual side that leads us to the hope of betterment. We hope things improve in our lives so that we become better as a result. We can hope for tough times to end, for loved ones to heal physically/emotionally/spiritually. We can hope to grow closer to others and even for simple day to day tasks that may seem arbitrary. It's all those little things that make our days full. I believe if we face difficult situations with faith, hope, and love, we will conquer them in a positive, victorious way.

Love softens the most hardened heart. I have learned to forgive others and remember that I need forgiveness as well. I need to acknowledge my mistakes, think about how I can make positive changes, and then apologize. I can do this with people and I can take this to Christ in my daily prayers when I sin against Him. He knows our hearts and intentions. If we come to Him with hearts of repentance and change, we are forgiven. The sins are gone. Sometimes it is me who cannot forget or forgive. I'm working on self-forgiveness just as much as I am working on forgiveness of others. I'm getting better at remembering that once I'm forgiven, it's gone. In this life, we don't tend to forgive and forget. We really need to focus not on earthly ways, but God's ways. I remember how much I am cared for and loved, and I can share that with everyone I know.

I have difficulty with unconditional love. I'd like to think that I love people all the time. I think we always need to be working on that. If we are sad or hurting, consumed by relational or individual situations, we tend to sit in that moment with those feelings. All of a sudden, our emotions can change based on something we just heard, the lack of effort, or differences in views. We need to remember that we are constantly loved in good times and in dark days equally, thus making it unconditional. God does that! We are here in His image, and due to imperfections and the nature of sin, we fall short of consistency in our time, effort, forgiveness, mercy, and love we give to people we know. I try to recognize my shortcomings. I try to stop my thought right in its tracks and change it to the positive. I remind myself that if I want to be forgiven, I need to forgive. If I want to receive love, I need to know how to continuously give it away, with no conditions. I tend to find myself shutting others out by getting quiet, with little to no responses, especially on social media. I refrain from liking and making comments and wonder what I can fix. In the past, I would act this way believing the one I was upset with would notice, even feel my silence. I realize now that I was trying to punish them, and that isn't up to me. As time passed, I was diligently trying to work on my spiritual journey. I am working on patience and love. I want to discern how I am feeling and why I feel this way without overreacting and responding defensively. This quiet time is now used to think through positive ways to change my negative attitudes and thoughts and find a constructive way to communicate with others in a loving way. I am learning to lean on God more and trusting Him to help me. I strive to speak to this person effectively so I can share my feelings without judgment, haste, or responding too soon. I'm learning to bring this to God in prayer more often throughout my day, even writing about the struggle on a piece of paper, which usually turns into a poem. In finding a way to get it off my chest in a positive and healthy manner, it becomes a forever reminder for me and a help to others. Often, I will walk in a nearby forest preserve, lake, or park. Being outside heightens my senses, as well as opens my mind up to discernment. I might not have the answer now, but I'm learning to be patient in the wait, relinquish control to God, accept His love, and be able to give it away. It isn't the perfection in the giving and receiving of love, but winning wisdom in the journey towards it. Sometimes we think we need to act in a grandiose way to show it. It really is in the simple ways, like smiling at someone, holding a door, stopping to help someone with a task, or just waiting with them until help arrives. We can send a card, offer a listening ear, give advice when asked, make plans, or simply sit with someone in quiet. These are small actions, but they last a lifetime for someone who needs you.

Faith, hope, and love work hand in hand, but love is the glue, the driving force for feelings, thoughts, attitudes, words, actions, and reactions. Through amazing times and those that are the most difficult, love truly exceeds above all else. It brings every part of our character to light. Love reminds us why we are here. It is love that creates and keeps relationships together. We focus on friendship, hope, family, work, strength, and fulfillment. We are reminded of what unconditional love really is and looks like through Jesus's life here on earth. We also receive that from Him now, and for an eternity in heaven. Do you know that no matter what you do, He will always love you? That love is so great, so powerful, and so wonderful. We feel a fraction of that at times and what seems like a ton at others. That is our limited understanding of unconditional love. His love is never failing, always abundant, and always on time. It is victorious over sin and death.

I hope you keep your hearts and minds open to the greatest love, the love that He has for you. He created you with a plan. He shows us how to love on, help, and teach others. It doesn't cost a thing. It's a free gift of the most ultimate love we can receive. He's just waiting for you to invite him in, to be your greatest friend, and lover of your soul.

Love is the glue to all relationships!

Blessings Abound!

Lisa Oddo

Lisa Oddo

Lisa Oddo is an educator of children with special needs at the elementary and middle school levels. She has a BA in Early Childhood Education and a Masters in Teacher Leadership. Both degrees were earned at Elmhurst College. Lisa has taught children of various ages, abilities, and needs for 27 years. It is important for her to help each child learn from the academic, social, and physical skills and strengths they have and use those as a springboard for growth. She is active at the local and regional level of the Illinois Educational Association for the support staff in her school district.

Lisa has always had a passion for writing and editing. She edited the short story *Misfortune* that was included in an anthology titled Eclectic Beyond the Skin. She also edited a novel titled *Relic of the Cross*. Lisa wrote about of the passing of her mother from breast cancer from her recollections as a child.

Her friend is culminating stories to help others who are coping with cancer in their family.

Lisa is very active at Bloomingdale Church, where she is a participant in the worship team, choir, Women's Break Bible Study, greeter, usher, nursery helper, and has more currently taken on the role of the Governing Board Secretary. Lisa is also an ordained minister. She has a position on her homeowner's association board and is a member of the Women's Club of Addison, a philanthropic group which focuses on helping women and children DuPage County, Illinois. She has served as president, Philanthropic Chairman, Recording Secretary, and Mayor's Charity Ball Committee Representative.

Lisa's future writing goals are to publish a book of poems she has written. She would like to include photographs she has taken of people and places that inspired these works.

Lisa Oddo
MissOddo@att.net

Amiee Boswinkle

Darkness, Darkness Everywhere

I regain consciousness to the sound of metal being crushed, the sensation of my face being smashed hard into an unknown surface, dust in my throat and confusion in my brain.

What happened?

Where am I?

What had I been doing?

My heart is racing, anxiety and fear loading up. My adrenaline is pumping.

What was I doing?

How did I get here?

I realize that I'm in my car. My airbag has deployed. I have just smashed the front end into a telephone pole.

My nose feels like it is bleeding. I start to cry.

A crowd of people has already formed. Someone is knocking at the window, "Ma'am, are you okay?"

I lock the door. My adrenaline is pumping, fight or flight mode kicking in. What is the escape route? Do I run?

I unlock the car door and make a beeline to the left, down a sidewalk.

I quickly realize I'm surrounded by people. People who heard the crash, saw the crash… I'm not sure what they saw or heard. All I know in this moment is I'm surrounded by people on all sides. It's like they are a safety net, all circling me and keeping me trapped in the middle. I try hard to divert a little further to the left; to break through, to run to safety, to hide and get away from the scene of my sin.

There are people everywhere! Asking me if I'm okay, if I need an ambulance, asking what happened. I run back to the safety of my car and lock the door.

I had been drinking. Again.

What am I going to do?

I hear the police sirens getting closer.

This will be my 3rd DUI.

My brain starts working: Where can I hide? There's nowhere to hide. I'm stuck in my car, surrounded by what appears to be a mob of people. I feel like I'm the main attraction at the County Fair, on display for everyone to see, gawk at and judge.

I'm a good person. Why do I keep doing such bad things? How do I escape?

I have no idea what day it is, where I am, or how long I've been up and going. Memories of the past 24 hours start to load up in fragments, but nothing makes sense.

I succumb to my pain: the pain of knowing the police are coming, I'm going to be arrested, and I'm going to go to jail.

Everything is a blur, but I remember bits and pieces.

I get arrested. I'm handcuffed. It's summer. It's sticky, hot and humid. I'm put in the back of the squad car. There's no air conditioning, so the back window is rolled down about ¾ of the way. We start to drive down the road.

I decide to find some way to kill myself.

I can't go to jail. This is my third offence; there's a huge possibility I'm going to jail for a year this time. I'm super flexible, so I curl my legs up in the back seat, lift my butt off the seat, and slide my handcuffed hands from the back side of my body to the front. I'm able to shimmy myself up onto the window that is rolled down.

We're driving down the road. I sit on the window's edge.

The policeman sees what I'm doing. He asks with astonishment and force, "What are you doing?"

"I'm going to jump out this window while you are driving and kill myself," I reply.

I don't even give him a chance to reply. I gently push myself backwards out of the window and land, hard, on the road.

I start to roll down the street. I'm still alive, but I'm in a lot of pain.

The policeman stops the squad car, gets out, and starts yelling at me. "What's wrong with you? What are you doing?"

I can only answer silently in my head. "I'm broken."

There's another side to me: a demon. The demon lived in the addictions. I became another person when I was using. Screaming, cussing; trying to kill myself; belittling everyone who came in contact with me. I could exude brute strength in this state of being, a strength many couldn't comprehend because of my small stature. The demon inside, who owned my soul, was strong and cruel and hateful.

We get to the police station. I'm belligerent.

They call an ambulance to take me to a Psych Ward: I'm too mentally unstable to be taken to jail at this point. I'm fighting, verbally and physically, with everyone. I'm a different person: I can see this, even in my state of drunkenness. *Who is this person? What's happening?*

I fight the entire ride in the ambulance. I'm shaking the entire gurney with my sheer will, trying to physically break free from the temporary prison of the movable hospital bed.

I get to the Psych Ward. I don't remember exactly what happened, but I'm sure I'm given a sedative to calm down and fall asleep.

A few days pass. I come to my senses. I totaled my car. I'm in the Psych Ward. I'm under arrest: my third offence.

My boss is made aware of my circumstances. I'm terminated from my place of employment. My boss tells me: I will never again hire someone who tells me they are in recovery.

I have nothing and no one. I'm alone, with my thoughts.

I'm released back to the police officer who arrested me just a few days prior.

My parents, from the kindness of their hearts, help me post my bail. They decide to let me back into their home one last time, under the condition I have a job while I am trying (AGAIN!) to put the pieces of my life back together. I have to find a job within walking distance from their home, because I have no car and they are, understandably, not willing to drive me anywhere. I know I had to have a job where I won't be missed too much if I leave, because I am sitting under the heavy weight of a court date and possible jail time.

Three blocks away from my parents' home is a health food store. I am hired.

September 2005, the entire trajectory of my life changed for the better.

I wish I could say I never drank again after this incident, but I would be lying. (As I am writing this now, it's been years since I have drunk alcohol. How many? I don't know. In reality, it gives me intense anxiety to keep track of sober days. Many people can keep track of sober days, and I deeply admire this. It just doesn't work the same way for me. There's a perfectionist part of me that loads up fight or flight reactions and obsession around this. So, I let it go. I'm backwards. When I look back on my entire life, I see how I have always been backwards from others. It wasn't a bad thing; just a different thing. Once I owned this, accepted it as just a part of who I am, life became easier.)

I loved the health food store, every single part of it: the people, the information, the customers. What I loved most was the knowledge the other employees shared with me.

I was learning new ways to heal. Ways that were not brought to my attention by my doctor, AA, NA, or my therapist. The prescription medications I had been put on made me feel numb: I could be in life, but I couldn't feel life. They made me tired and zoned out. I felt like a zombie.

For the record, I am not against AA, NA, doctors, therapists or prescription medication. In fact, they help a lot of people, and I am genuinely happy for this. I'm just saying that they didn't work for me. All I share is my own personal journey of experience, strength and hope.

I began to learn about protein and amino acids and how they heal the human body; the human mind. I began to drink protein smoothies every morning, and I gained clarity. My cystic acne began to improve. I lost 10 lbs. My skin tone improved. I began to sleep at night. My anxiety improved.

Slowly, I began to feel better. I began to feel and be alive again in the world.

I came off my prescription medication. I started taking a multi-vitamin. I felt even better. I had more energy. I felt renewed.

Who was I becoming?

I began to study the human body on my own: how structure and function work within the mechanics of the human body system. It was fascinating.

I learned about Candida, and how this type of yeast overgrowth can be a culprit for alcohol cravings, acne, sugar cravings, headaches and much more. I tried a Candida cleanse. I felt better!

Every new thing I learned, I applied to myself. I became my own guinea pig. (I don't advocate my approach to people with ill health without consulting with their doctor first.)

I began to question: why had I never been educated on nutrition from my health and wellness providers?

I was learning how important food was to heal. But medicine for me also came from exercise and adequate sleep, practicing self-care, and learning how to tune in on my body's personal stress signals and what they meant. Perhaps these were things some people learned, but the people I encountered over the 12-plus years at the health food store didn't seem to know much about this approach either.

So, I taught people my approach. The protocol I used to heal my own self.

Sugar and carbs contribute to the blood sugar roller coaster. Candida contributes to yeast overgrowth. Inflammation causes distress internally. Digestive distress contributes to further illnesses in time. Too much fight or flight response causes adrenal fatigue, and wears the body's energy system down.

Soon, I knew more than the others at the health food store. I educated them as much as I could about what I had learned. I educated people on how their bodies worked. I told people to keep their doctor in the know, and to ask their doctor if this might work for them too.

As I got physically healthier, I knew I had to heal the inner demons I held inside: shame, fear, guilt, blame. I had played the role of victim for so long, I knew I was an Academy Award-winning actress in my heart for the game I was playing.

I lived in shame for so long—shame of my past, of the things I had done, of my DUI's, of the people I hung out with—that no one really knew me.

One day, 11 years into my journey at that health food store, I shared my life with my co-workers. No one had known the pain and trauma I had endured in my lifetime. Some cried. Some were in awe. Some felt like they were sitting in an AA meeting. Everyone, including me, left that day different.

I left empowered. I became a new person. I re-designed myself. I stood in the powerful truth of who I really was: a person who knew how to teach my approach to people suffering from the pain of trauma, PTSD and addictions, and help them break free from the prisons of their own minds.

Now, I work for myself; something I never thought possible. This journey I am on has taken on a life of its own, and I am grateful for this opportunity.

I've only just begun. I know that my story will be a catalyst for great change in the trajectory of human health care.

Amiee Boswinkle

Amiee Boswinkle is a Certified Health Coach and an Intuitive. Amiee found her way out of the darkness and into the light after debilitating trauma, PTSD and addictions took over her life. When she couldn't find reprieve from conventional health care or therapies and all hope seemed lost, she took matters into her own hands and studied the human body until she was able to heal herself. Today Amiee touches the hearts and lives of people suffering from trauma, PTSD and addictions. She helps them break free from the prisons of their own minds through her 1:1 work with clients and sharing her story of experience, strength and hope through public speaking and workshops.

Amiee has a B.A. in Psychology from Ball State University, is a Certified Reiki Master Teacher through the teaching of Pamela Kozy at Heart In Hand, and is a Certified Health Coach through Health Coach Institute. She has been a guest speaker on the 2017 Global Health Care Symposium "Creating Infinite Health," a guest speaker at Unity of Northwest Indiana and Unity in the Dunes, and has spoken three times as a guest for the Facebook group Beyond the Limits Summit.

Amiee desires to heal the wounds of the weary and lost through her teachings. Her goal is to uplift the vibrational energy of humanity with the wisdom acquired through the lessons of her lifetime.

"Fear has created separateness in our world. The connection we are seeking is love. Infuse the world with you, your truth and your essence, and ignite the fire necessary for change. Love will change the nation. The nation starts within you." —Amiee Boswinkle

Amiee Boswinkle
Connections Restored
1637 N. Indiana Place
Griffith, IN 46319
219-793-3889
amikboz@yahoo.com
www.ConnectionsRestored.com

Tina Guimar

Tragedy to Triumph

I was a broke, overworked, struggling accountant with ambition and the desire to succeed… until everything came crashing down in my personal and professional life. I found myself taking on way too much so I could prove I could move up the corporate ladder.

Over twenty years ago, I was a young mom with no college degree and working three part-time jobs, when I was offered a full-time position in accounting. I accepted the position and found I was good at it. I didn't love accounting, but it was paying the bills and providing health coverage… and I needed a career. I started at the bottom of the corporate ladder and realized I needed a piece of paper to prove I could advance. I wanted to be a manager, but as we are all taught growing up, you have to have the proper degrees to go anywhere in life. It didn't matter that I had the experience and was already doing the job. I started attending college part-time at night while working full-time and raising my family. This lifestyle went on for about fifteen years.

Who was I trying to prove anything to, anyway? There are certain beliefs instilled in us all throughout childhood… that we must go to school, get good grades, get a good job, get married, buy a house, have kids, and work very hard until retirement. Me? I did everything backwards. I had kids, bought a house, went to college while having a good job, and then got married, and was well on my way to working very hard until retirement.

I always put everyone else first and never took the time to take care of myself. I got to a point in my life where I hated who I had become. I was exhausted and run-down. I was sick and tired of living life in emergency mode, always running from one thing to the next. Until one day... I had a real emergency.

It was Easter 2015. We had just arrived at my parents' house for Easter brunch when our neighbor called to tell us our house was on fire. Boy, was it a long ride back home. An hour with all kinds of things going through our heads... only to get home and have to stand in the street, not knowing the real damage happening in the back of the house. After what seemed like hours in the freezing cold, we were allowed to go to the back of the house. When I saw what the fire had done to our home of fourteen years and all of our belongings, I nearly fell to the ground. Devastation hit me like a ton of bricks. My heart was shattered into a million pieces. Everything we had was gone in the blink of an eye. I had no idea what was to come. Where would we go? What would happen now? Why was this happening to us? Luckily, many people came together to help us. We are forever grateful to our generous family, friends, and even strangers who helped in many ways.

To my surprise, this was not the end of the tragedy. There were many more events in store for us before things would start to get better.

I continued to push through instead of taking a leave. Work always came first. I even continued to work toward my MBA while living in a mobile home on our property, for eleven months during the rebuild. It felt like everything was a battle... every interaction and every conversation. How many more things could we possibly deal with at one time? I had no idea what I was doing, but I would figure it out... just like I had figured out everything else prior to this.

Then, my husband woke up sick one day and could no longer work at his job. We lost half of our income. He visited several different doctors, for months and months, and had almost every test under the sun, and still we had no answers. So, we would just adjust to a new way of living. No big deal... we had already been through the worst, right?

Meanwhile, things were falling apart at my job. Everything I had worked hard for up until that point seemed like it wasn't enough. Changes were being made in the company, and I had become so comfortable that I had not seen it coming. I was not happy with the decisions that were being made and found myself wanting out of my job of ten years... the job I always said I would retire from. I found myself questioning if I was even in the right career.

So, I did it... I resigned and took a position as an Accounting Manager. It was the very position I had longed for, because now I had the title. The commute was longer and the culture was far from what I had been accustomed to for the previous ten years. I felt like I was trying to change who I was as a leader just to fit in with this new environment.

A few months after I started my new job, my father-in-law passed away. I became tired and drained; then I found out I was anemic and had to go for treatments to get my iron to the right level. A couple of months later, my grandmother passed away. My heart was breaking for my family, but I kept pushing through. Two weeks later, I received the most devastating call from my father in the middle of the night. My brother was gone... he had taken his own life. How could this be happening? Hadn't my family been through enough in such a short period of time? Would I ever wake up from this nightmare? He had been so happy, and had been a totally different person since he met his fiancée. What the hell was going on? There were so many unanswered questions.

At that moment, I knew it was time: time to stop trying to be so strong, and time to swallow my pride. It was time to ask for help.

So I did... I went to the doctor. I was diagnosed with anxiety and depression, put on medication, taken out of work and referred to Cognitive Behavior Therapy (CBT). I had always joked I would end up at Butler (the psychiatric hospital), and there I was taking day classes to learn techniques to get me through rough times.

It was at this time when I learned about mindfulness and meditation. During my sessions at CBT, one of the therapists said something that really hit home. He said, "If you are not being yourself, you are in the wrong place." Wow!! What a huge light bulb moment for me. Mindfulness, meditation, and the rest of the CBT topics helped me get back on my feet. I truly believe CBT should be taught in schools from an early age. Forget about this lifestyle of living a fast-paced life where everyone is miserable; we really just need to slow down and be present in the moment as much as possible. It is time to enjoy what little time we have on Earth.

For two years following the fire, I had been stuck in a merry-go-round of a nightmare. I had became angry, bitter and closed off. My anxiety became so bad I could hardly control my emotions anymore. I was miserable at work, at home, and everywhere in between. I was either raging mad, crying my eyes out, or complaining about everything. I was in a constant state of negativity, and everything under the sun bothered me. I ruined so many relationships with my constant negativity. There were days where I did not even want to get out of bed... but I knew my family needed me.

How would I fix this? I knew something had to change, but I did not even know where to start. So I began my search for a better way. I knew there had to be a way to experience true happiness and fulfillment, because I could see other people were living the life of their dreams. This was when it dawned on me: I had forgotten to dream. I made the decision that I was going to become the person I was meant to be.

I hired a mentor and went to work, learning how to be successful in Network Marketing. I had been in and out of Network Marketing for about fifteen years with little to no success. I decided it was time to get serious about this industry, because I knew there were top leaders who were helping many people. What was their secret? I always had an entrepreneurial streak, but I did not think I could go off and open my own business when I had responsibilities. What a huge limiting belief it was. I have come to learn you can achieve anything you set your mind to, if you have the proper mindset and the proper tools and resources. Always remember: 90% of success is mindset and only

10% is skills.

I realized I had lost my purpose, passion and drive. Who was I? My mindset was terrible and I had developed many limiting beliefs. I spent many months getting into the right mindset and found my passion in helping others. When I had been in a supervisory position, I enjoyed helping my staff set goals and objectives and helping them be successful. This was the part of my accounting career I absolutely loved. I also loved finding new ways to make processes more efficient. Now I get to help others reach their goals and objectives, while also helping them create efficiencies so they can have the time freedom they deserve.

Once my mindset had improved, I still felt like there was something missing. I did not like begging, chasing and convincing people they needed to buy what I had. So I started my search for the missing piece. I've found it in an amazing community of people where I have learned everything about online marketing. I have found my home, where leaders are being created every day.

What I want to leave you with today, based on my experience, is this: make sure you are doing what you love, take time for yourself and your loved ones, be present as much as possible, always be authentic, follow your heart and chase your dreams. Times can be challenging, but if you remain focused and keep moving forward you will get to whom and where you are meant to be. Time is going to pass anyway. All you need to do is make a plan and take action. Be open to new ideas, be ready to transform your life, and learn to embrace change. Be creative and not competitive. Have patience with yourself. You are worth it! The sky is not the limit... the only limits are the ones we place on ourselves.

The formula for success is to focus on the following steps every day:

• Practice meditation and visualization

• Connect with the right people

• Work on personal development

- Learn something new

- Execute what you have learned

I have always been a firm believer that everything happens for a reason. Sometimes we do not realize why things happen until later. Little did I know, everything that had happened in those few short years was a result of what I had been putting out into the universe. It was everything I attracted to me. It is so important to understand how the Law of Attraction works, because it will make you or break you.

My mission is to make an impact and change many lives, now and for future generations. I recently came across a journey compass charm bracelet, which is a symbol of guidance, adventure, inner strength, and dreams. It is a reminder to live life to the fullest and trust your journey. Your best adventures lie ahead.

Tina Guimar

Tina Guimar is a certified transformation life coach who helps women handle change with grace and balance. She utilizes techniques from her mindfulness life coach certification in her coaching program. Her focus is to help her clients realize their true potential, live life to the fullest, and trust their journey. She encourages them to gain clarity on their passions, interests, values, core beliefs and strengths. She guides her clients to work smarter, not harder, by creating efficiencies to allow for true time freedom.

Prior to her new journey, Tina was in the accounting industry and holds her Master of Business Administration. In recent years, Tina experienced drastic change in her personal and professional life after a tragic house fire and other major events. She was climbing the corporate ladder, until she realized her heart was not in it anymore. It was not until later when she found that her passion lies in helping others achieve their goals.

Tina is the co-founder of Elite Ladies Network, LLC, whose mission is to empower women to Stand Up, Stand Out, and Stand Proud in life and in business. Elite Ladies Network, LLC was formed to create an online community of like-minded women who are on a mission to make an impact. The founders believe it is extremely important to support other women who are on similar journeys. It is nearly impossible to be an expert in every field or in every area of business. Elite Ladies encourages their members to leverage each other's talents, enabling them to experience expanded networks and increased business.

Tina is a wife and mother of two adult children and two Cavalier King Charles Spaniels. She is a native of Rhode Island who likes to travel and experience different areas. She enjoys personal development, reading, meditation, music and playing pool during her downtime.

Tina Guimar
Elite Ladies Network, LLC
Hope Valley, RI
401-290-7072
Tina@EliteLadiesNetwork.com
EliteLadiesNetwork.com

Debora Rogers

Beating the Odds

It's funny how many different people we can be in one lifetime… I know I've been at least a dozen or so…

I was raised in our local Assembly of God church. We went as a family until I was about twelve years old. After my father stopped attending, we all stopped, one by one. But I continued my relationship with my Lord and Savior Jesus Christ.

I never felt like I fit in anywhere. I always thought I was adopted. I always felt like I was living someone else's life, like I didn't belong where I was. I felt like I had nothing going for me, no special talents or blessing. No value. My older brothers were the smart and funny ones. My younger sister was the pretty one. I was just Debbie.

I was the kid being bullied by the cool kids. I was never one of the popular kids in school, or the prettiest, or the smartest, or even the funniest. In P.E. I was always the last one standing, and a team had to take me. I can't say how many times in my early life I felt like I was, or wanted to be, invisible.

My Dad broke his back at work when I was fourteen years old. We were thrown into devastating poverty. We had never been "rich" but we'd had everything we needed. I had always had a hard time in school, and having to wear "hand-me-downs" and thrift store clothes at that age compounded things. My science teacher called me Raggedy Ann and laughed at me. I felt like a loser and a real burden.

When I was fifteen years old, I was in a bad car accident. I couldn't go to school with a broken leg and a fractured skull. I had double vision, so I had to hold my head tilted to see straight until I healed.

Only three months later, I married the driver of the car.

My mother asked my husband-to-be two days before our wedding, "If things don't work out, then what?" He said, with a shrug of his shoulders, "We'll just get a divorce, I guess." I didn't understand that he was serious.

I was sixteen with a husband and a house to manage! I was also trying to figure out what I had gotten myself into. I had to figure out how to pay the bills and balance a checkbook, quick.

He waited two whole weeks after the wedding before he started a fight with me so he could go out. I didn't see him again until the sun was coming up. I blamed myself. I couldn't understand what I had done to be treated this way. It was his plan all along. He loved his games.

Fast forward seven years later... It was New Year's Eve. We had talked about going out, so I started dinner early and arranged a babysitter for the night. I was thinking he should be home early from work so I wanted to get dinner done early. I had never made stuffed bell peppers before. It was a lot of hard work, but I expected the payoff to be worth every minute. He got home early all right, and brought a friend from work with him. Turns out they had got off work at noon and had been in the bars all afternoon. He came home only to trade the company vehicle he had been driving all day for his hot rod.

Shortly after he left, I received a phone call. It was his friend's girlfriend informing me my husband had hit a house with his car just down the street from their house. She said, "I don't know if he's dead or alive."

He lived... and I left!

It was the last time I would allow him to treat me that way. I was done! We divorced! The divorce was ugly, it seemed to go on forever! I remember wondering if I would ever be free of him. He promised to kill me every time I saw him.

A year after I left, my 1971 Mustang Mach 1 was stolen from my driveway. I loved that car! It was found a week later in an almond orchard; the engine transmission and interior were stripped from it and it was burned. My ex-husband was arrested and prosecuted for the theft. We were STILL waiting for the judge to sign the final decree.

I found myself a single mother of three at twenty-three years old, working two jobs, with no car and enough guilt to sink a battleship. Their father wasn't meeting his financial obligations, so I had to step up and make up the difference. The worst was not being able to give my children everything they needed.

I saw families coming into the restaurant where I worked with their happy kids, ordering anything they wanted to eat. I was shocked at how others were able to have anything they wanted while I couldn't manage to pay my electric bill until it was dire straits. I wasn't even able to take my kids to the zoo for a day trip. How were these people able to have new cars and nice clothes and take vacations? It opened my eyes to the fact that not everyone was struggling like I was! I knew there had be a better way or an easier way to make money than the path I was on. I was trading my time for money.

I realized these people had their own businesses. So that was my next step! I made some calls and signed up immediately with a friend in a network marketing company. I was told not to worry; I wasn't alone, and I could call her anytime I had a question... But the only time she knew my name was on order day. It was a constant struggle. I made my list of 100 people and still struggled.

Many years later, I joined another network marketing company. My upline was great. We became good friends, and I loved working with her and her upline. I did everything I was told to do. I bought and used drop boxes in businesses to get leads. I bought leads and cold-called people I didn't even know. I put up flyers and bandit signs and I plastered my link everywhere. I attended every company meeting! I spent hundreds at the copy store! I did everything they told me to do. I had a little success, and yet I was deeper in debt. I had only a handful of people on my team and they were dropping like flies!

I remember one day asking my upline after we had been out recruiting, "When do we get to stop doing this?" She said, "Never. If you want your business to grow you will always be replacing people that fall off." I couldn't imagine doing this for the rest of my life. I asked, "But how do people build huge organizations?" She shrugged her shoulders.

I did have some success early on. I won trips to Las Vegas, Pismo Beach, California, a luncheon cruise on a yacht, and a trip to Montego Bay, Jamaica. And many, many Sales Awards.

Then my upline passed away suddenly. Her upline passed away the following year. My manager, whom I loved and who had helped me set and achieve my goals, ended up changing jobs. My struggle returned.

I always knew there had to be a better way! An easier way! I went on a mission to find it.

It's been my experience that as women, we tend to be the dumping ground for our families. We usually keep everything bottled up inside, or we talk to a friend. Here is one technique I've learned to release myself from the pain others have caused me. I write a letter to the person and put words to all my pain, then read it over and over until there's no longer emotion tied to the words. Then I burn it or shred it; just get rid of it.

We as a society, I feel, are always worried about what others think of us. There's a saying I heard a few years ago: "If you knew how often people really think about you, you'd be surprised, because they really don't!" This was HUGE for me.

Throughout my life I've always been drawn to personal development books, audios, videos, YouTube videos, and attending live trainings and events. I probably have 1000+ books and audios. I decided I needed to hire a mindset coach, and I found one that had been personally trained by Jim Rohn. I personally worked with him for over a year to help me get my head straight. He taught me that the difference between success and failure is only about six inches (the distance between my ears.) My success or my failure both start as a thought in my head. He taught me about meditation and the benefits of having a vision for my life and business. He said we are all creators: we create our own world and everything in it. Everything in our lives is there because we have attracted it to us. I knew then I had created my life the way it was, so I could also create the life I wanted. Since then, I've had many coaches and mentors.

It's the little things we do daily that make the difference! You must have a vision for the life you want. Ask yourself these questions:

- Where do I want to be in one, five, and ten years?
- Who do I have to become to get there?
- If I could do anything I wanted and money wasn't an obstacle, what would it be?

Then make a plan! I heard a wise man once say, "If you don't yet have the business you want, it's because you haven't yet become the person you need to be to build, maintain and grow that business."

I struggled with depression and dark thoughts for most of my life, until I was healed at a live event. Now I believe my depression was unused potential. I hadn't allowed myself to push through the mind blocks and limiting beliefs. Our minds always tend to go to the negative, if we let them. Now I fill my mind with things like meditation, music and positive thoughts. Our brains' main goal is to keep us safe. When we step out of our comfort zone, we feel unsafe, so naturally our brains want us to pull back. Don't! Keep moving forward! If you don't plan your life, you'll fit into someone else's plan for their life.

For the first time in my life, I found a way to attract the right people to me. I didn't have to chase, convince and beg people to buy what I had. It was so liberating! As they say, "the rest... is history!"

I want you to know you're not the first person to struggle and/or not know what your passion is. It took me years of struggle to find my passion. I took the long road. But I still arrived! Now I have my vision for my life, and my future, and nothing will stand in my way of achieving what I choose. Don't let anything stand in your way. It's worth the struggle! You deserve success! If no one has given you permission to be successful, let me be the first!

It's so rewarding and amazing for me, when I can help a person that's struggled like I struggled. Suddenly they understand what they've been missing. It's a miracle to watch! It's the difference between day and night for them. It's my passion!

The most important asset we have is our time. Once it's spent it's gone forever. So, I thank you for your time. I hope you find value in my story and learn from my mistakes. I look forward to connecting with you and helping you.

Debora Rogers

Debora Rogers beat steep odds as a young child. Although she didn't have a storybook childhood, she persevered. After becoming a young bride, within a few short years she found herself a young single mother. Overcoming many obstacles and facing her trials head-on, she has proven to be a survivor and a warrior.

Today, she holds certifications in Transformation, Entrepreneurship/ Business, REBT Mindset, and CBT Cognitive Behavior life coaching. She helps her clients through transformations in their personal and professional lives, through reigniting their dreams and desires and identifying their ideal paths, to achieving their goals and regaining control of their destinies. She helps each client gain clarity and define their passion, values, strengths, interests, core beliefs, and how to stop blocking their success. She helps them stay focused on what matters most, stay motivated, and stay accountable. As a second love she teaches marketers how to attract more buyers.

Debora is the co-founder of Elite Ladies Network, LLC, whose mission is to empower women to "Stand Up, Stand Out, and Stand Proud in life and in business." Elite Ladies Network, LLC was formed to create an online community of like-minded women who are on a mission to make an impact. The founders believe it is extremely important to support other women who are on similar journeys. Since it's nearly impossible to be an expert in every field or area of business, Elite Ladies are encouraged to leverage each other's talents and expertise, enabling them to experience an expanded network and increased business.

Debora has been remarried for twenty-two years. They have a blended family with six grown children, ten grandchildren, ten grandpups and five canine fur babies of their own. Over the years they've rescued numerous homeless or abandoned dogs, rehoming most, while some have become part of their family.

She enjoys reading, coaching, teaching, yoga, music, the ocean/beach, Chinese food, hamburgers, and ice cream sundaes.

Debora Rogers
Elite Ladies Network, LLC
Porterville, CA
559-920-0818
Debbie@EliteLadiesNetwork.com
www.EliteLadiesNetwork.com

D. L. Navarro

We Are Built to Survive: My Life of Trials, Tribulations, Terror, Tragedy and Transitions

To get a feeling for what my entire life was like, is simply described as being on a rollercoaster going as fast as the speed of light. It would slow down, it appeared I was getting off, and whoa, hold on, here I go, it would slowly pass the exit and kick into high gear. Here I go again.

Being married to a raging cocaine addict was the hardest thing I have ever done in my life. At the same time, the job I was best at was being a wife. Yes, I stood by my man. I loved him. The unfortunate part for the addict is people see him for his disease. It is only by a mere gift of sobriety that you can see through to the real person buried inside of themselves. If that day ever comes.

I was born and raised in a small bungalow in the neighborhood of Bridgeport in Chicago. I was an only child. My dad was a tool machine operator, and Mom babysat six children. When I was three years old, my grandparents moved to Wonder Lake in McHenry County to pursue their dream of the country life. We were left behind to take care of their family — my great grandparents and uncle, who was an alcoholic. We ran for everything they needed. It was a lot of Italian drama, as the grandparents constantly fought. My Uncle Joe Joe would get thrown out of bars and we would be there to pick him up out of the gutter, a bloody mess.

What I found out 39 years later, seeing my first therapist who happened to be an addiction specialist, was that this learned dysfunctional behavior as a child, taking care of others and trying to fix them, is where I started my codependent career which would forever change my life.

Little did I know that I was about to kill myself out of my own life. My mission for the rest of my days were spent on doing what I learned best. To save Marty.

It wasn't until my parents moved us from the city to the western burbs that I finally got him away from his degenerate friends in the ever-changing hood. Then he got his new job, and ready, willing and waiting was a new group of suburbanite kids with high-grade drugs. This is what sealed Marty's ill-fitted fate forever. The party boy turned into a full-fledged addict.

From that day on, fear, panic and pandemonium drove me off the deep end. Talking logic to him, begging him, and laying down ultimatums. I was thrown into the depths of darkness, seclusion, and exclusion.

First an accidental overdose and then a drug-induced accident landed him in the psych ward. Thankfully, he would be on his way to the first 30-day rehabilitation. I dropped him off and will never forget him standing, looking out the door's window, crying. Seeing him tore me to shreds. I could never do the "tough love" thing.

Sunny days seemed ahead. He was going to Alcoholics Anonymous/Cocaine Anonymous meetings, but never grasped the 12-step concept. The open meetings taught me their sayings and I adopted them as the philosophy of my life. The black cloud was looming, with more relapses ahead.

After high school, my friends went to college to get degrees to become secretaries. I hated school, so I went right into the workforce. I was getting free, on-the-job training for the companies I worked for. I had great jobs: AAA Chicago Motor Club, Blue Cross Blue Shield, Associated Aviation Underwriters. I finally got a job in the western 'burbs and no longer had to commute downtown.

I hated my cubicle. I was a people person. My duty at Coldwell Banker was to hire cleaning services for all of our 60 centralized offices. I became friends with our main service, good old Jack. Despite hiring cleaning services, the thought of me cleaning never crossed my mind. I would sit there and dream about being self-employed. I would say to myself, *How would you do that? You're not a scholar! It takes money to make money, and you don't have money. What do you know how to do?*

Meanwhile, Mom went to the dentist, and he asked her how things at the hospital were. She said she wanted to leave the job she adored in the newborn nursery. Babies were all being born addicted to drugs. He asked if she was going to go back to hairdressing, and she said no. He asked her what she wanted to do, and she said, maybe clean offices. He told her to pick up the key on Tuesday. Mom picked up the key. After our day jobs, we got in there and did what we did best: clean. After all, growing up with Mom, cleaning our little bungalow was an everyday passion. Vacuum and mop every day. She had a reputation in the neighborhood. They'd say you could eat off Rosie's floors!

This would be the inception of Mrs. Clean Office Cleaning Specialists. It was Mom's nickname on the block, a no brainer. But we were only cleaning one office. The three of us thought this was cool. Marty and I thought it would be great to have another office to clean. It didn't take long for me to apply every single aspect of all I had learned at all my jobs. My office closed down. I went to work for a regular Coldwell Banker real estate office with realtors. This is where I learned my lion's share, marketing, contracts, canvasing and had flyers from cleaning services trying to get our business.

All the stars aligned for us. I knew exactly where to start and what to do. We wrote ads, went to the printer, and walked our asses off in office parks, shoving hundreds of flyers into mails slots for miles. The next day, we received two phone calls for bids to clean their offices. *Oh. My. God.* We were flying on adrenaline and excitement. *Now what? What do we do when we get there?* We winged it, just let them talk, and we answered questions. We couldn't get far like that. A light bulb went off and I had my very first networking contact help me, I had good old Jack's business card. He had no problem consulting with us. After all, a wise person would know there was enough business to go around for everyone.

We started building clientele and had to get past the disappointment of pounding the pavement and getting no calls. We worked day and night. We finally got to the point where we all quit our day jobs. Quickly, fear kicked into high gear for me. I had to deal with customer complaints and applicants who were bottom of the barrel workers. After all, I learned anybody worth hiring had a good job already! Ha!

This business turned into a safety blanket to keep Marty away from himself. Now I had two gigantic monkeys on my back. My cocaine addict who wouldn't stop, and the business that had its typical ups and downs. We moved out of our little mobile home in Countryside and into a huge house in Naperville. Status had us. Marty was still at it. One day, after coming down from being high in our library, he said, "Debbie, I'm not going to do this anymore." The Codependent's response: "Yea, I wish I had a dollar for every time he said that!"

Well, Marty meant it. The next six years he was sober and flourished as the businessman he was meant to be. He was a risk taker, not I. We had no luck getting help. We worked seven days a week, no days off, worked on holidays, and never a one-week vacation. All work and no play would make Marty a depressed boy.

A huge set of unfortunate circumstances would plague us. Psychiatrists were booked out six months.

Marty relapsed before he made it to the doctor. We were never apart. Together 365 days, 7 days a week, 24 hours a day. We were soulmates and thrived on being together. To this point, I had seen nothing yet.

Have you ever had your worst nightmare come true? I have. Recovery says that doing drugs you'll either end up insane, in jail, or dead. In one short year, he nailed all three. The last year of his life was a war on drugs inside my own home. Drug dealers deliver to the burbs. Behind closed doors and our white picket fence lie the pain and torment inside.

And it was the end of us.

That fateful day, I woke up to Marty collapsing in our bed. I was on the phone with 911. Once they arrived, I watched my husband die in front of my eyes. I watched them not save him… I wet my pajamas from this horror. As they rolled him on the gurney down our hallway, I told him everything was going to be all right. They didn't bother to tell me he was gone already.

Mom and Dad had raced over. The ambulance never turned its lights on and left after what seemed like forever. While gathered at Edwards Hospital they put us in a little room. Mom didn't know what had happened at the house. I had a sick feeling this room was not good. The doctor came in, sat, and started asking me what had happened. I started to tell him. My mother stood up and shouted, "Did my son-in-law make it?" He sat there, heartless, and said, "No, he didn't." A lump in my throat dropped and I felt strangled. I swear my heart was frozen in that moment. I stopped breathing. People rushed in, holding me, begging me to breath. I didn't want to anymore. After all, I watched him die in our bedroom.

You never expect to hear the word no.

Looking back on that year, I could clearly see how God prepared us to be separated for the first time. What you are going through today is preparing you for what lies ahead. You can pray to God for the outcome you want, but whether you like it or not, you may just suffer a tragedy. Going at the speed of light around the clock, it was either him or me who was going to die that day.

Twenty-three years had gone by, and in the back of the hospital with my husband, as he lay there turning blue, I finally got it, I was never meant to save him, and I was playing God.

There I stood, looking off the edge of this earth all by myself. I had some choices. I could sell our home, business, move back home, and pursue the dream of what I should have been, a psychologist. I decided to keep going with my independence I gained from the past year. Keep doing what I knew best: working our business. I didn't want to live. There was a hole in my heart, bleeding profusely in my thoughts. Every night after work I fell listlessly to the floor, wallowing in a river of my own tears.

At Martin's wake, oddly, people were telling me now I could grow the business. I said I couldn't do that with him alive, much less alone. They gave me some sort of karma. That year, I doubled my business. With all the new business, I hired my protégé.

I was at my client's desk to write a note, saw a stack of cleaning service cards, and I called it. It was Rhonda, my employee who tried to steal my clientele. Firing her put me into desperation. I had more work than help. I would set out to find a trustworthy replacement.

I sit here a better person for living through all the torment one life can take. Being a young widow at 39 was the first of many transitions that I would be forced to endure. As I say, "Life has a way of dragging us through, even if we're kicking and screaming."

Mrs. Clean Office Cleaning Specialists was nominated by a construction company we worked for and named one of the Top 50 Construction Cleaning Companies in 2009. We were featured in the *Illinois Construction Review* trade journal. How exciting! The excitement came to a screeching halt when the recession hit, and I lost half of my business from struggling companies.

Then I was audited by the IRS, right out of the hospital after hysterectomy surgery. My accountant abandoned me, and I was forced to conduct my audit at my dining room table alone.

I never seemed to regain my footing rebuilding the business back up. I started to drown in bills. I was in over my head and headed for a possible foreclosure on my home. I put it on the market and nothing happened. I was stuck.

Business made an upturn from the accolades of our award. I was in a constant race to interview employees to help me with all the new business. In the meantime, my health was on the back burner. Eventually, this long-lived lifestyle would challenge me physically and mentally, and ultimately leave me disabled.

We are built to survive even the worst tragedies, and you may even find that the best days of your life are ahead of you. People who come into our life are not always meant to stay. Which pains me to say that to this day.

Overcoming mediocrity my entire life was in part due to my core values and strengths: patience, perseverance, persistence, and a promise. I'm a victorious woman for never giving up. I had unintentionally manifested through God and the Universe, throughout my life's prayers and mantras to having arrived at my answer for purpose. To reinvent myself to fulfill my dream on this journey, as I sit here becoming the author I was meant to be.

D. L. Navarro

D. L. Navarro is the CEO of Mrs. Clean Office Cleaning Specialists. Mrs. Clean was founded in 1988 by Rosemarie S. Thomas. They are celebrating 30 years in business and is a proud partner and member of www.homeadvisor.com. Mrs. Clean was nominated and awarded Top 50 Construction Cleaning Services in Illinois in 2009 and was featured in the *Illinois Construction Review.*

Deb attended the College of DuPage for business classes. In four short years, right out of high school, all of her various jobs would make her an autodidact. She, of course, excelled in the school of hard knocks.

Martin Michael Diaz, Deb's late husband, died so that she could one day live the life she left behind 23 years ago. Deb is actively involved in coaching clients in grief, relationships, and entrepreneurship. She is thankful for www.soberrecovery.com. Without this site, she may not be here. Help is only one click away. Through sharing the pain of loss with other addicts, many have held on, if only one more day.

Deb is happily remarried to Raymond. The night they met was kismet. He is an officer, a gentleman, and is a wonderful caretaker with Deb's complete disability. When she met Raymond, she thought that was the happy ending of her story... but she learned that it's just the next chapter.

Deb's words to live by are engraved on a 40-year-old plaque that hangs in her den:

"Do what you can, and then pray to God to give you the power to do what you cannot." –St. Augustine

Deb credits the book *When Bad Things Happen to Good People* by Harold Kushner for being the catalyst that made her move past her grief and get ready to celebrate the journey of finding her own identity.

    *Lifetime Member Cleaning Management Institute
    *Member BOM Building Operation Management
    *Member of IMS International Monetary Systems
    *Member Contracting for Profits

D. L. Navarro
Mrs. Clean Office Cleaning Specialists
Darien, IL
630-712-3324
DebMrsClean@yahoo.com

Valerie Roman

Victory Reimagined

Every story needs a beginning. Mine begins when I was born, in 1956—a baby boomer—and grew up in Somersworth, a small town in New Hampshire. My dad worked at the local factory, my mom was a housewife, my sister was eight years my senior, and we had a lovable beagle named Cookie. It sounds like a postcard picture of Americana in the 1950s, and in many ways it was. I remember, in the evenings my family would watch *The Donna Reed Show* together, noting how Donna just seemed to solve all of her family's problems, all of the time. The show provided us with a prototype of the perfect woman. Donna was happy, calm, and beautifully dressed (including pearls). She was a college graduate and a former nurse. She cooked, baked, ironed, kept an impeccably clean and organized home, and constantly tended to the needs of her husband and children. Many years later, a humorous episode of the *Gilmore Girls* described Donna Reed as the quintessential 1950s mom with the perfect 1950s family: never without a smile and high heels; with hair that would crack if you hit it with a hammer. Unfortunately, many women, including my own mother, felt a sense of inadequacy when comparing themselves to Donna Reed.

As I reached my teenage years, I realized that I was becoming a bit restless in my postcard New Hampshire town and began to wonder what else was out there. This made me begin to think about how I might fit into that world. Also, for the first time, I had to confront the fact that, beginning at a young age, girls are provided with various prototypes of the perfect woman—a Barbie doll, a television or movie star, a world-renowned athlete, or a supermodel. As they grow older, girls continue to confront unrealistic ideals of who they are supposed to be and what they are expected to do to be successful. The image of the perfect woman may have changed over time, but its existence has remained constant. How could I, as a small town girl, ever measure up?

Having done well in high school, I was able to attend Wellesley College, a prestigious women's school in Massachusetts. There I was urged to strive for excellence, be a leader, and make a difference in the world. I often wondered if I could succeed. After all, Wellesley College had graduated so many women of achievement — Secretary of State and Senator Hillary Clinton, news anchor Diane Sawyer, Secretary of State and U.N. Ambassador Madeleine Albright, and National Public Radio commentator Cokie Roberts, just to name a few. No pressure there. At Wellesley College, I majored in math and economics. This probably had something to do with the fact that people said they were "hard subjects for girls".

So when I reached young adulthood, I realized that I wanted three things in life: to take care of myself and live a long, healthy, and happy life; to have a successful and satisfying career; and to raise a happy family and be the best wife and mother I could be. I also recognized that I wanted these things on my own terms; not any idealized terms, and not anyone else's terms.

I then came up with a novel way of thinking about these three things I wanted in life. When you grow up near Boston, you can't help but become an avid sports fan. I have followed all the Boston teams passionately. When a player on my favorite ice hockey team, the Boston Bruins, scores three goals in one game, it is called a hat trick, and fans celebrate and honor the player by throwing their hats onto the ice. As you might guess, scoring three goals in a game is quite an accomplishment. I came to think of accomplishing my three primary goals as scoring my personal life hat trick. However, I did not want to suffer from — as I called it — the Donna Reed Syndrome. I did not want to seek perfection and set myself up for a feeling of failure.

My mother and father successfully raised a happy family. However, they did not take care of themselves and died at a young age, never attended college, and thought in terms of jobs rather than careers. I realized that to score my personal hat trick, I would need help. So, for the next thirty-five years, I researched and gathered tips and tricks from everywhere I could that would help me past life's next hurdle. I took an empty hatbox from my mother's closet and began to stuff it with the best articles I could find for becoming the successful, fulfilled person I wanted to be. I began to fill the hatbox with magazine and newspaper articles on topics ranging from eating sufficient fiber in my diet, to organizing closets, to asking my boss for a raise. My mother, a suburban housewife, could not teach me all I needed to know to become a successful "Do It All" woman. I had to learn that on my own from what I read. And it worked. As the contents of the hatbox grew, so did my belief that I could succeed and score my own hat trick.

After graduating from Wellesley, I was offered the opportunity to work for the Census Bureau in Washington, D.C., to learn computer programming at the government's expense. After racking up steep student loans during the previous four years, I was thrilled they actually were going to pay me to learn new skills. And I had always lived in New England, so the idea of experiencing another part of the country was alluring, although a bit daunting. I told myself I would go to D.C. for one year, but ended up staying there for seven years. During those years I met my future husband, got married, and had my first son. I also had the opportunity to work for the federal government in the Jimmy Carter and Ronald Reagan administrations, which was wonderful for a young woman. The government was well ahead of the curve when it came to inclusive language. I learned words such as "chair" instead of "chairman" and "staff resources" instead of "manpower." I appreciated the flexible work schedule offerings. I was treated equally and was provided numerous training opportunities not only in technical training, but in management training as well. The concept of a woman manager seemed very natural there, and I had many women as role models and colleagues. I climbed the career ladder quickly and before long, became the director of systems analysis and design. My job at the Census Bureau was the keystone to my long and happy career. It prepared me well for my next opportunity: to be the first technology director for the City of Cambridge, Massachusetts.

I left the programming job in Washington not only for the professional growth opportunity, but also to move back to New Hampshire and bring my son closer to his grandparents. A definite win-win situation. Although the City of Cambridge (affectionately called "The People's Republic of Cambridge") is a progressive city, at the time I was there, most power positions—such as city manager, assistant city manager, finance director, human resources director, and budget director—were filled by men. It was a wonderfully enlightening and rewarding time, and provided the opportunity to be a trailblazer on two unexpected fronts. First, no woman had ever participated in the office football pool and, when I was let in, I was asked if I picked winners by the color of the team's uniforms. As an avid sports fan, I found great joy when I won the pool! Second, I got pregnant with my younger son three years into my tenure and needed to collaborate with the human resources director to update the employees' manual, since I was the first department head to ever become pregnant!

After twelve years, I left Cambridge and took a job as director of technology at the esteemed preparatory high school Phillips Academy in Andover, Massachusetts; not only for the career opportunity, but also to cut my commute in half and to provide my sons the opportunity to attend there. It was as if I had taken a 180-degree turn. Many of the top power positions at Phillips Academy—head of school, assistant head of school, dean of admission, and human resources director—were filled by women. Again, I was blessed with many role models and mentors.

I have worked full time professionally all my adult life, with the exceptions of a six-month break after giving birth to my first son and a three-month break after giving birth to my second son. Whether I was at the Census Bureau, at the City of Cambridge, or at Phillips Academy, I had long, stress-filled workdays that came with long commutes in rush-hour traffic. Every job has positives and negatives, but focusing on the positives is important in pushing through the hardships and finding each job more fulfilling in its own way. I am proud that I was able to break a few barriers for women in the male-dominated technology field. I was five feet tall in a world of six footers. It was difficult, but one of the perks was that I never had to wait in line for the ladies' room!

When I reflect back, I often think of an influential time early in my career. I attended a management seminar that required us to write down a list of five people who had most influenced, supported, and impacted our lives. Of course, I listed my parents. I also listed my favorite high school teacher, my supervisor and mentor at the Census Bureau, and a friend of more than 50 years. After we completed our lists, we were asked, "Now think about people you manage. Would any of them put you on their lists?" This seminar had a profound impact on me. From that moment on, I have focused on having a positive and lasting effect on other people's lives. I have told this story to several people, and it has brought me such happiness when many have written to me, "You are on my list."

Finally, when I was fifty years old, it hit me. I had actually accomplished my personal hat trick: I liked myself and was healthy and happy; I had a great career; and I had a terrific husband and had raised two terrific sons. I was victorious! It was not the victory of becoming some model of a perfect or super woman; it was not a victory defined by others; it was my victory on my terms.

I have realized that the information I gathered over 35 years of moving up the career ladder, finding happiness with my husband and children, and enjoying life to its fullest has helped me so much, it might help other women find their victory. After all, it was a sifted assembly of my own experiences and great advice from many magazines and newspapers—*Better Homes & Gardens, Eating Well, Family Circle, Family Fun, First for Women, Glamour, Good Housekeeping, Ladies' Home Journal, the New York Times, O the Oprah Magazine, Parenting, Prevention, Professional Woman's Magazine,*

Psychology Today, Real Simple, USA Today, Vogue, Woman's Day, Women's Health, Working Mother—as well as books, websites, and television shows, such as *The Doctors* and *The Dr. Oz Show*. Many of the pearls of wisdom I had kept saved me from the various perils of life, ranging from wearing the wrong earrings for my facial structure, to not getting enough vitamins in my diet, to hiring a loser for a job.

So, I recently published a book titled *Hat Trick: The Essential Playbook for Career, Family, and Personal Balance* to offer my lifetime of lessons, my stockpile of struggles and successes, and my years of relentless research. I hope the book will help other women on the challenging, but always fascinating, journey to score their own hat trick in life, whatever that may be—and to become the best version of themselves that they possibly can. Visit www. ValerieRoman.com for more information.

Valerie Roman

Valerie Roman was the director of technology at Phillips Academy in Andover, Massachusetts, where she also served as president of the Eight-Schools Technology Directors Association. Before joining Andover's faculty, she was the first information technology director for the City of Cambridge, Massachusetts and served as the vice president of the Massachusetts Government Information Systems Association. Under her leadership, Cambridge became the second city in the country to introduce a website and electronic city hall. Prior to her success in Cambridge, she was the director of systems analysis and design for the U.S. Census Bureau in Washington, DC.

Valerie has also been an active member of numerous professional associations, including: the National Association of Female Executives, the Business and Professional Women's Foundation, the Massachusetts Municipal

Association, the International Society for Technology in Education, and the American Association of University Women. Her accomplishments have been recognized in The Wall Street Journal, ComputerWorld, and the Boston Globe.

Now semi-retired after more than 30 years as a technology manager, Valerie provides consulting services to municipalities and schools. Valerie graduated Phi Beta Kappa and summa cum laude from Wellesley College, with triple majors in mathematics, economics, and education. She recently published a book titled *Hat Trick: The Essential Playbook for Career, Family, and Personal Balance,* a fun and fact-filled playbook about juggling family, career, and personal well-being. Visit www.ValerieRoman.com for further information.

Valerie Roman
Municipal Resources, Inc.
32 Blossom Road
Windham, NH 03087
603-432-3733
VRoman@aol.com
www.ValerieRoman.com

Dorothy Hawkes Cavers

The Evolution of a Dream

I'm a baby boomer whose love affair with corporate America has changed! The promises that were made have been broken. The opportunities that were lost forced me into living an unexceptional life, not good, not bad, just mediocre. I've opened my eyes and I know if I want the future I deserve, I must reclaim the dream, my dream, the American dream of a full and fruitful retirement and financial freedom!

My story starts in the early 60s, on the heels of the Civil Rights Movement, on the New Jersey coast, in the shadows of the bright lights of New York City. I was raised by my maternal grandmother, in the hood: urban to some, suburban to others, but always home to me! There was a strong sense of pride growing up; in my family, in my community, and in my town. I grew up in a loving dysfunctional family which was part of a bigger, racially segregated, dysfunctional community. Quite honestly, I'm not even sure how I ended up here, because the odds of winning at life were stacked against me, not from birth, but from conception.

Hood life is a hard life. For me, education—which started with Head Start—was my ticket out of the hood. I was blessed to have found a mentor in a guidance counselor, Mr. R., who worked hard to expose me to all educational opportunities that could help lift me out of the hood. He wanted to see me succeed. Not just me, though; he wanted education to lift all the youth in my community, where positive role models were rare and a life of government assistance or personal injury lawsuit damages was the primary source of income for most families. I wanted to rise above the poverty. I wanted to be someone, have nice things and not have to lie about how I obtained them. More importantly, I didn't want to disappoint Mr. R., for he was the only stable male figure in my life. He wanted the best for me; even if I didn't know what that was, he did, and he believed in me! I was the first one in my family to obtain a college degree. It gave me a sense of pride that carried me through the decades.

In 1980, I was going to be a rising freshman at a prestigious all-girl private college in New England, a place far from what was familiar. As I was preparing for my high school graduation, I remember sitting in our kitchen appreciating the sights of neighbors talking, sounds of children playing, and smells of multicultural foods being prepared for dinner. I vividly remember my excitement upon hearing the latest news: the new retirement age was 55! According to the numbers—and you know numbers don't lie—after I got my degree, got a job, saved money and paid my taxes, I could retire in 2017 at 55!

I did what was I was told to. I had the degree, I had the career, and I paid my taxes… But I'm still working, with no real end in sight, because something changed. That something was the retirement age that needed to be reached to receive "full benefits". The retirement age kept getting older: 55, 57, 59, 62, 65, and now 67!

With sadness, shock and anger, I watched the years change and my dream of a comfortable retirement become even harder to reach. I am mad! I feel cheated and lied to! I realized years ago that Social Security was not going to be what I needed it to be, and that I would need to find another way to fund my retirement. But I didn't know what that way would be, or if I could even reach it. I had an Associate of Science degree in Fashion Merchandising and Management, and a Bachelor of Science in Business Administration, so I felt armed with formal education, and street smarts! I was going to be someone that made a difference in the world!

I started my career off in retail. It took less than six months of working nights, weekends, and holidays for me to realize this was not the career I wanted. That's when I discovered corporate America. I loved everything about it: the hours, the benefits, the security it provided, and the opportunities for advancement. I was giddy with excitement. The thought of having nights, weekends and holidays to spend with my family was intoxicating! I thrived in this environment as a triple threat: female, black, and educated. Corporate America loved me... Until it didn't.

Was it good? Yes, it was. It was a love affair for the record books, and experiences for which I will forever be thankful. But today, and certainly tomorrow, it's just not enough. I look at my life and I feel conflicted; how is it that I own real estate and cars, I take great vacations and help my family and my community, yet I am unfulfilled.

Currently, I am one year past my promised retirement age, and I feel compelled to do something different or risk being unhappy, with no time or money to enjoy retirement. I am building my legacy. I'm going to make good on that retirement promise.

I've had four long-term employers during my career, and I am thankful to them all individually and collectively for their part in the blessings that I have had in my life. My first long-term job was for a farm and garden cooperative and lasted for four years. When I went to human resources and expressed a desire to move up in the organization, they told me there was no place for me to go. So, I resigned and went to work for a bankruptcy court. It was a temporary job that lasted six years! It was an amazing experience that provided a platform for the transferable skills I had within me to flourish. When that job ended, I moved across the country to work for an arbitration company. I stayed there for six years, until I was unwilling to relocate to a rural community when the corporate office moved. I found my last corporate job on Craigslist. It was a match made in heaven; I had everything they wanted, and they had everything I wanted and more. It was perfect. I was in a constant state of bliss for nearly 20 years! Honestly, I never thought of life outside of corporate America, because I loved it, and believed that it loved me!

Going through menopause changed everything in my life, from how much sleep I got on a nightly basis, to what clothes I could wear. If I had a hot flash in public, the question was, would I be able to stay fully clothed until it passed? My hot flashes were so out of control that at any point in any day, I could be dripping in sweat to the point that I had to change clothes. If I was in public strangers would look at me sympathetically, because I looked ill. Store clerks constantly offered me a glass of water, a seat, or in a few instances, asked if I wanted to call the paramedics. Too many times I was mortified at how my body betrayed me. One of the most embarrassing moments was when I was conducting an educational seminar for a medical group of 30 physicians and their staff. During my presentation I began to sweat profusely. I tried to ignore it by wiping my brow (this was before I started carrying a fan and a handkerchief) and silently said, "I wonder if they can see me sweating?!" Not only did they see me sweating, the physicians stopped the program until I could regain control of my body.

Menopause also brought emotional problems, which led to me being treated for anxiety, depression, and insomnia. All three were treated with medications that had nasty side effects. I was dependent on medications to help me make it through the day, yet the side effects were making it impossible to get through the day. It was the longest and darkest period of my life. To make matters worse, my love affair with corporate America was being challenged.

In October 2018, I was reintroduced to network marketing, direct sales, and the dream of financial freedom. I had tried Amway in the 80s and Herbalife in the 90s, so I was familiar with the opportunities direct sales provided for those willing to work for it.

It was through my search for a solution for my decade-long ailments of hot flashes, leg cramps, and night sweats (all unavoidable symptoms of menopause that women generally were not talking about), that I found a solution to a lot of my problems. My search led me to a company whose products literally changed my life overnight. The first night I tried a new product to ease my menopausal symptoms, it worked! I had no hot flashes, and no leg cramps or night sweats. I woke up well-rested and felt like I had been given a new lease on life. I no longer take any medication to help keep my mental health balanced. My blood pressure, which was treated with medication, has been normal since October 2018. I have mental clarity that I did not have prior to trying all-natural products, and I can say without hesitation that the quality of my life has improved greatly.

I researched the business opportunity and made a decision that altered the course of my love affair with corporate America, and gave me a purpose. That purpose is to help other women realize their full potential, help them become home business owners, and/or improve the quality of their lives by eliminating the symptoms of menopause that make everyday activities a chore. I have realized that I have been given a rare gift of experience, and that I have a duty to share what I have learned with others who may be suffering. We can make life altering decisions that lead to monumental changes, if we are willing to move beyond our comfort zone.

For so long I had given up on my dream. I had resigned myself to living a mediocre life where there was never enough time and money… at the same time. Living a life where my schedule was dictated by others. Living a life where I acted as the middleman between my employer and my creditors, because I never had any money left over for living. It's a sad existence for this woman who played by the rules and did what I was supposed to. Yet I still couldn't live the dream promised so many years ago. I have realized that timing is everything! As a corporate sweetheart I was not familiar with how to be a successful entrepreneur; however, lack of knowledge will not stop me from investing in myself and in my dreams, and helping others along the way. When opportunity knocks, we not only have to answer the door; we must step in, grab a seat, and create our destiny!

I'm sashaying into my future with attainable early retirement goals! I want to invite other menopausal baby boomers to sashay with me and realize the full potential of their dreams.

When is the last time you thought about your dreams? How are you doing with your retirement plans? Are they on track? Can you see yourself retiring at an age where you can enjoy the fruits of your labor? Are you paid what you're worth? Has your dream evolved to include a new chapter?

Dorothy Hawkes Cavers

Born and raised in New Jersey, Dorothy realized early on that education was the key to avoiding a brutal cycle of cultural marginalization. Her education started with Head Start, which led to her becoming the first one in her family to earn a college degree. She studied Fashion Merchandising and Management in New England and graduated with a Bachelor of Science in Business Management. After a short stint in retail, Dorothy chose a career in Corporate America.

Dorothy became a Corporate Sweetheart who thrived most when helping others to achieve professional and personal objectives. While working for Dalkon Shield Claimaints Trust in Richmond, VA, Dorothy began to realize her gift as an orator. She took advantage of every opportunity to progress. During this time she became one of the most successful alternative dispute resolutions representatives who were representing the Trust in binding arbitration hearings, and also trained staff to do the same. Dorothy served as a certified court-appointed family mediator for the Supreme Court of Virginia and became an acclaimed platform speaker and resource in Alternative Dispute Resolution and medical malpractice arenas.

Currently she works as a risk manager for a physician-owned insurance company, and conducts communication workshops for physicians on disclosing unanticipated medical outcomes around the country. Her dream is to retire from Corporate America and enjoy retirement with money and time, at the same time.

Dorothy Hawkes Cavers
Cavers Attraction Network
15335 Washington Avenue, #307
San Leandro, CA 94579
510-290-9663
TheCaversAttraction@gmail.com
www.CaversAttractionNetwork.com

Carol Rambo

My Life Song

LIFE ON A PEDESTAL

As a kid, my mom always put me on a pedestal. She would say to my little sister, "Why can't you be more like your sister?" Being seen that way meant that I had to toe the line and make sure I was always the good girl who never got in trouble. That is where my perfectionism had its roots. After all, I certainly did not want to fall off the pedestal.

Mom ruled the roost. She had a way of making my dad feel badly about himself. One night when we were sitting around the dinner table with others, she said something mean, and my dad started to cry. He said, "It's OK. You will never understand how much I love my Millie." I saw dad "suck it up" over the years and deemed him a true "saint." I so wanted to be like my dad. But I didn't understand then that trying to be like a "saint" would lead me into co-dependency and leave me unable to set healthy boundaries.

Overall, I was very blessed with loving and giving parents who were always there for me and supportive of all that I did.

THE GREAT DECEPTION AND BETRAYAL

During my college years, I fell for a man who was unlike me in most ways. I had a false belief system that said: I can certainly help him to be the man I want him to be; and most of all, I can most assuredly help him to be a Christian. I was under a great deception. My thought was, "If only I can be perfect, then he will always choose me."

One of the ways I thought I could be a perfect wife was by making fabulous meals for us and gourmet meals for company. I would work on these meals for several days, just to impress. The table was always set elegantly. However, there was always a cold chill in the air. I never knew if I would get a thumbs-up or a thumbs-down. Sometimes my ex-husband would throw food across the table. One time I spent hours making a gorgeous cheesecake. When my ex-husband tasted it, he gagged and spit it out and said, "This is not the kind of cheesecake that I like." My friend said later, "I can't believe you didn't just smash it right into his face!" Looking back now, I would love a do-over on that one. I think I have come to a place where I would totally enjoy smashing that cake in his face.

When my ex-husband saw me without makeup for the first time, he asked me if my face had gone down the drain. You can guess how many times, in 20 plus years, I ever let him see me again without having makeup on.

He was a womanizer, plain and simple. He cheated on me before we were married and never stopped after we were married. Wherever we went, his attention was always on all the other women around us and never me. Even in a restaurant, it was all about the waitress.

I knew when we went out I had to look as gorgeous as possible. Once I got all glammed up and felt like I looked great, only to come downstairs to one of his negative comments: "Your eyebrows are not even." Seriously?

Once I had spilled a little bit of drink on my dress. He said it was too embarrassing for me to be seen like that, so I had to stay put at the table. However, a little bit later, after he had gotten drunk—something he seemed to do every time we went out—he decided he wanted to dance. He threw me under his legs, and I ended up scooted across the floor on my back with my shoes flying in opposite directions. Since this was at an event at a Catholic military academy where my son attended, I was mortified!

It is one thing to feel guilt over not doing something right or well enough, but it is quite another to experience shame because of who you are. Probably the worst thing I had to endure was constant rejection in the bedroom, because of his pornography and adultery. It started the day after our honeymoon and continued the entire marriage. I would not be able to count the nights that I cried myself to sleep over those 24 years. Rejection led to shame, which led to more perfectionism. Surely there is something I can do… But nothing worked. I guess there must be something wrong with me…

He was also sexually abusive to our daughter. He used to look us both up and down, and even compare our body parts. He acted in extremely inappropriate ways; but he was that way with all women, so it seemed logical in my mind to excuse that type of behavior. Besides, I never wanted to rock the boat.

He would not let me open the door at night when my daughter had a night terror and came screaming and pounding on the door. Because of my own fear of my husband, I would obey him. Thus, my daughter remembers feeling that I was never there for her. Consequently, my daughter deals with feelings of inadequacy and never measuring up. That is something that we are working through, even today.

We also have a son, who seems like he survived living in this type of family. Yet, when I ask him if he remembers things, he seems to have little or no recall about anything we did as a family; not even our fabulous camping trips to Colorado. He has become a huge success with his company, and I am so proud of him. But deep down, I think he is still trying to prove to himself— but even more so, to his dad—that he does measure up.

My ex-husband's promiscuity and unwanted sexual advances extended to my family, friends (even good friends), and customers who would come to our home when I was gone. And the saddest part is that no one ever told me. Some even knew about his affairs, but their excuse for silence was, "We don't want to hurt Carol." Seriously? What do you think causes more harm: knowing or not knowing? My advice to anyone would be, if you know that this kind of perversion and behavior is going on… PLEASE SAY SOMETHING! My children and I might have been spared from many years of abuse.

He chose many women over me for all of our married life. And then he found a woman he chose permanently. One day "it" arrived: the letter in the mail. It contained a sentence formed with words cut from a magazine or newspaper, stating that my husband was having an affair. (Their relationship had been going on for many years.) I found out later that this letter came from the husband of the woman he was seeing. So, look who I had to get the truth from!

Thus, our marriage of 24 years ended. My self-delusion and co-dependency kept me believing that he would come back to me. One blessing came out of this waiting period: I did not date, so I had plenty of time to heal and understand my own sickness.

SINGLENESS AND SUCCESS

During the last 17 years of our marriage, something came along that helped me get healthy, not only physically but also financially and emotionally. God used a time of suffering (about three years of deteriorating health, extreme fatigue and constant migraines) to take me to a place where I could truly help others regain their health.

I received my certification in nutritional counseling from a nutritionist whose classes and teaching took me to a place of more credibility in my field. I found I loved teaching people about nutrition, getting them on the right program, and seeing their health improve. Thirty-eight years ago I was doing what was almost impossible. I was trying to tell people that what they use to wash their clothes and clean their house has a direct impact on their health and the environment; it was a new idea. And to try to help others understand that food supplements were a way to fill the nutritional gap caused by the way foods are grown—that was almost heretical! Yet there were always those who believed me. As I began to lecture in homes and churches, my organization was slowly being built and lives were being changed.

Because of my involvement with multi-level marketing companies and their superior products, I became successful in helping others do what I was doing. Because of God's favor and faithfulness in my five years of singleness, I never had to find a job or worry about how I was going to make it. During those five years, I was getting a new car every two years. I was able to travel to Hawaii, Italy, Switzerland and the Netherlands with my son, and spend three weeks in Spain with one of my sisters, as well as visit really cool cities all over the United States with my daughter.

One thing that is taught in MLM is the beauty of passive income, even during retirement years. Never discount the truth of that. You just have to find the company that gives you purpose and reason for doing what you do. And the knowledge that the hard work comes first, and then, with willingness to always be there for your people, the benefits will remain.

THE JOY OF SECOND CHANCES AND MOTORCYCLES

Thus enters my iron worker Rambo man. It all started at the Cadillac Ranch, where a friend invited me to go line dancing. I loved dressing up in glitzy clothes and a fancy cowgirl hat and boots! And I really loved the dancing!! But after I had been going week after week and never had a dance partner, it was a welcome gesture when they asked all the singles to step into a big circle. That's when I met Tom. We became permanent dance partners, meeting two to three times a week at the Ranch.

Our first date outside of the Ranch was to my church, Willow Creek Community Church in Barrington, Illinois. Tom liked it, but would come and go and constantly resist any work of the Spirit of God, who was trying hard to get his attention.

One day, God did get his attention. He had been an iron worker most of his life and never had an accident, even 60 stories up in the air. But one day God used a mighty wind which almost knocked him off the beam, and he really got scared. That, coupled with hearing a country western song on the radio that same night about "coloring inside the lines," was his wake-up call. And that very night he surrendered his life to Jesus Christ.

And everything was peachy keen after that, right? Wrong! That was just the beginning! We both seemed to have a love for motorcycles, so we borrowed one to try out. On the way home, a deer ran out in front of us. To keep the bike from crashing into it, Tom inadvertently put his leg down to stabilize the bike. Long story short, he shattered his leg like a twisted toothpick. He was told by the surgeon that he would be lucky to walk and would never be an iron worker again.

After six months of therapy, prayers, and lots of supplements, he walked me down the aisle. He went back to work shortly after that—yes, as an iron worker, back up on those beams!

We enjoyed our early years of marriage on various motorcycle trips. We would be gone for three to six weeks at a time, covering most of the United States and Canada.

A couple years later, I accepted a volunteer position with the Willow Creek Association as a Placement Coordinator. My responsibility was to place pastors from all over the world—every nationality and culture—into homes of people who volunteered to be a host family, usually for a week at a time. For many years, the WCA had five or six different conferences a year, so it seemed that I was working in this capacity throughout the entire year. Tom and I also served as a host family for all of these conferences. Over the 20 years that we served in this capacity, we had the privilege of helping more pastors/leaders from all over the world than I can even recall. To this day, we keep in touch with most of them. We enjoy looking at our guest book, filled with many kind comments, remembering and being thankful.

As a side note, my old Alma Mater, Lutheran High School East in Cleveland, Ohio, is always looking for very important people to put on their Wall of Fame. Included were doctors, engineers, teachers, lawyers, and other people who had made huge impacts in their fields. My sister submitted my name, because of my work as a Placement Coordinator for churches around the world. I was actually chosen that year for making a difference in a global sense. Alas, I have never been to see that wall!

Tom and I celebrated our 25th anniversary in October. With God's grace and a healthy lifestyle, we can still enjoy life and our Harley at age 75! Being with Tom is freeing. He thinks I look totally fine without makeup, he never criticizes my cooking (even if it doesn't turn out very good), and I never have to feel shame or rejection in any way.

TRAGEDY AND LOSS

Between the ages of 60–70, I experienced the biggest losses of all. My daughter's second child got a rare form of leukemia at age seven, and was on chemo and antibiotics every day for three years. In the midst of it all, her appendix ruptured. No one thought she would make it. That would have been enough, but because of a very evil man—her father—the entire weekend she was in the hospital near death we were not allowed to have any contact with them. We literally had people praying all over the world, because I knew so many pastors through my involvement with the WCA. By God's grace, she made it. She is almost six years cancer-free.

But that was not the hardest part of this decade. There is a difference between a bad person and a truly evil person, and "evil" is how all of us describe my daughter's ex-husband to this day. My grandchildren and my daughter feared for their lives every single day. I will not tell of the horrors they experienced, because that is not my story to tell. But I can tell you how it affected me. One day when I was sitting for the kids, he came and snatched them right out from under me. They left kicking and screaming. I felt helpless. Shortly after that, my daughter told me she had orders that I was not to see my grandchildren again. I was not allowed in their home, and they could not come to mine.

Grandchild number three had a birthday in November, and I wanted so badly to sneak a birthday present over to him. It was a cold and blustery day. I crept up the driveway and knocked gingerly on the door. My daughter opened it a crack, and her husband was inside. My grandchild came out in the cold, and I got to see him for a couple of minutes. Then he quickly opened his gift and ducked back inside. Outside of that, I had no contact with them for over a year. Lisa lived in a state of high anxiety, and totally under her husband's control. Being unable to see me or even talk to me was more than both of us could bear. She said that her daughter having cancer was not as hard on her as surviving and protecting her kids.

The day came when I was finally allowed to see my grandchildren again and have them over. One day, the father showed up and tried to take them away as before. My daughter and Tom were also present. I finally "put on my big girl panties" and grabbed the hands of two of my grandchildren. When he came up to me, all big and puffed up and threatening, I screamed, "You will never take these children from us again." We called the police, and they showed up and made him leave the premises. Since then, I have only seen him a couple of times — and that was in court.

My daughter and grandchildren moved in with us when we were in the midst of selling our home and moving. I was able to buy a house for them in a safe and lovely area. It was a much needed brand new start for them, and they are very happy and thankful to be living there.

Unfortunately, the father does not send any child support or alimony, and no one has been able to find him. However, God has continued to prove Himself faithful to this precious family. At the ages of 18, 16, and 15, my grandchildren are some of the neatest and most loving people on the face of the earth, superseded only by their mother.

CONCLUSION AND NEXT CHAPTER

I know that my story does not have the same punch as others. I have read stories of women going on in life to reach new heights and do great things to inspire others. I know that my plaque on the Wall of Fame stands pale in comparison to those others'. But if you ask my husband, my daughter and son, and my grandchildren (we have 15 altogether as a blended family, and 3 great-grandchildren), I think they would all say that you don't have to be famous to be valuable or inspirational. All you need to do is make a difference in the life of one, to change the trajectory of his or her life, and you become a hero to that person. And what more important place to do that than with your very own flesh and blood?

I would like to pass on some truths I have learned over time that might be helpful to others:

One: If you know something is wrong, please tell the truth to the person being affected. Don't let fear of rejection, or fear of hurting the other person's feelings, get in your way.

Second: No one can change another person — so give it up permanently! Leave that job to God.

Third: Refuse all fear. Choose courage in order to execute a rescue plan to save a person or family member held captive by evil.

Fourth: Have solid boundaries dealing with what is not acceptable in your life. Have a specific plan to protect those boundaries.

Fifth: Walk boldly through all open doors of opportunity that God brings into your life.

My next chapter is yet to be written. However, since God knows and holds my future, and directs my path every day, I don't have to know what it is. All I need to know is that all things really do work together for good to those that are called according to His purposes. My response is to surrender, trust, obey, and love Him.

Carol Rambo

Carol Rambo (better known as Rambette—more later) has a passion for helping people regain their health through personal consultations and recommendations. She studied underneath a nutritionist and is certified as a nutritional counselor. Since referring people to products of excellence is key in her consultations, Carol has been working with two different multi-marketing companies for the last 38 years.

Passion usually springs from a personal need or crisis, and that's where hers began, in her late thirties. Carol went through a horrific divorce in her late forties, but because she had built her business strong, financially, she was blessed and not busted.

God loves to give second chances, and hers included a Rambo (actual name) Harley motorcycle man. (Thus Rambette became her Harley signature).

She discovered the fun of wearing leathers and seeing almost the entire United States and Canada by motorcycle! With their blended families, Tom and Carol have 7 children, 15 grandchildren, and 3 great-grandchildren.

Most of what Carol has learned has come through a school of hard knocks. Her passion continues to be nutrition, but also pointing people to a God who is filled with grace, faithfulness, and forgiveness; the One who heals body, soul, mind and spirit.

Carol Rambo
3002 Talaga Drive
Algonquin, IL 60102
708-280-6370
carolrambo4@gmail.com
www.immunotec.com/healthycells